Knowing How

Researching and Writing Nonfiction 3–8

576 strategies clincher?

Mary C. McMackin
Lesley University, Cambridge, Massachusetts

Barbara S. Siegel
The Hardy School, Arlington, Massachusetts

Stenhouse Publishers
Portland, Maine

For Jim, Jimmy, and Katie
MCM

To my husband, Richard
BSS

Stenhouse Publishers
www.stenhouse.com

Credits
Pages 63, 68, 89, 92, 94, 101, 107, 108, 109: From *National Geographic for Kids!* Reprinted by permission.
Pages 54, 62, 63, 64, 65, 66, 70, 71, 72, 81, 83, 87, 88, 102, 103, 106, 108, 110, 111: From *Time for Kids*, a Time, Inc. Company. Reprinted by permission.
Pages 61, 86, 99, 100: From *Boys' Life*. Reprinted by permission.
Page 82: From *National Geographic World*. Reprinted by permission.
Pages 85, 90, 93, 102: From *Animals*. Reprinted by permission.
Page 105: From *Ranger Rick*. Reprinted by permission.
Page 109: From *Cricket*. Reprinted by permission.

Library of Congress Cataloging-in-Publication Data
McMackin, Mary C.
    Knowing how : researching and writing nonfiction 3–8 / Mary C. McMackin, Barbara S. Siegel
    p. cm.
    Includes bibliographical references.
    ISBN 1-57110-340-6 (alk. paper)
    1. English language—Composition and exercises—Study and teaching (Elementary) 2. English language—Composition and exercises—Study and teaching (Middle school) 3. Exposition (Rhetoric) 4. Report writing. I. Siegel, Barbara S. II. Title.

LB1576.M32 2002
372.62'3044—dc21   2002075754

Cover photograph: Photodisc/Vicky Kasala

Manufactured in the United States of America on acid-free paper
08 07 06 05 04   9 8 7 6 5 4 3

Contents

Preface

Imagine that you assign a research project to upper elementary or middle school students. They generate important research questions around issues that interest them. They collect data that relate specifically to their questions. They organize information and write reports that show passion for their topics and new content knowledge. None of the reports begins with "My report is about . . . [topic]" and none ends with "I hope you liked my report." Each one starts with a lead that hooks the reader and each provides the reader with a logical sense of closure—nothing is just tacked on at the end. In between, there are transitions that link one idea to the next and move the reader thoughtfully through the report. Wouldn't it be wonderful if all students wrote reports like these? They can. But before they can, they need to have a clear understanding of the task and concrete strategies to use along the way.

A few years ago, we began to explore ways in which we could help Barbara's fifth-grade students improve the quality of their nonfiction writing. At the time, Mary, an associate professor at a nearby university, was spending one day a week working with Barbara and other teachers in her building. Barbara was rethinking how she approached the research project with her students and Mary was eager to become involved in this process.

We know that students sometimes perceive the task of researching and reporting to be something different from what teachers understand it to be. A study by Schwegler and Shamoon (1982) confirmed this. They found paradoxical answers when they interviewed college freshmen and their instructors to see why they write reports. The students viewed this "close-ended" task as a tool to show off their library and documentation skills, as "an exercise in information gathering, not an act of discovery." Instructors, on the other hand, perceived research to be "a process of inquiry, problem-solving, and argument, not simply an information-gathering process." They expected students to "explore some aspect of the world and to make verifiable statements about it" (pp. 817–24). Schwegler and Shamoon noted that these contradictory perspectives often led to frustration for students and instructors: students were disappointed in their grades and instructors were dissatisfied with the quality of student work. Many times, upper elementary and middle school teachers feel this same sense of dissatisfaction with the quality of their students' research papers. They spend weeks, sometimes months, working on researching skills, only to receive papers that parrot back information, lack voice, and contain a string of scattered facts.

After experiencing similar frustrations, we embarked on a mission: to find what was missing in this process. We needed to understand why students were working hard and yet producing lackluster, formulaic reports. In order to find answers to our questions, we knew we needed to experience what the students were going through. So, we each selected an animal to research. We worked alongside the children, simultaneously teaching and learning each step as we went. This allowed us to observe what the children were doing, to model research as an inquiry process, to share our challenges and accomplishments, and to gain confidence in what we were doing as we waded into uncharted waters.

Along the way, we faced numerous challenges. Both of us struggled to help students organize their work; to find resources that were accessible for them; to write papers that displayed knowledge of their subject, as well as researching/writing skills and a passion for their topic. We turned to available resources for guidance and information: professional books and journals, professionals in the school (Title I, librarian, etc.), and colleagues in the field. Often, however, we needed more concrete support than was available. We needed to know how writers created expository texts.

We spent hours in children's libraries, collecting examples of effective writing that included interesting leads, transitions, and conclusions. After gathering a variety of samples, we analyzed them to understand what strategies the authors used. Next, we wrote a description for each strategy. We recalled that Barry Lane (1993) gave each of his strategies a name (e.g., "Snapshot," "Thoughtshot," "Explode the Moment"). We decided to follow a similar model. Attaching a name to each strategy helped the students concretize the abstract ideas and allowed us to give specific suggestions when we conferenced with them. As this process continued, the students became more empowered, and we continued to be impressed by the quality of their work. They now had strategies that gave them the confidence to take risks and experiment.

Knowing How: Researching and Writing Nonfiction 3–8 is designed for preservice and inservice teachers. It is organized into two major parts. Part 1, "Researching," focuses on the research process, from selecting a topic to writing a first draft. In Chapters 1, 2, and 3, "Getting There From Here," "Journeying from Topic to Research Question," and "Transforming Their Ideas into My Ideas," we set the context for the book and then walk through the process we use to help students select a topic, differentiate between "big" and "little" research questions, design personal data charts, and then use the information on the data charts to compose a first draft.

Part 2, "Revising and Assessing," focuses on improving and evaluating student report writing. This section begins with an overview of the process we used to collect and analyze exemplary leads, transitions, and conclusions.

In Chapters 4, 5, and 6, "What's the Connection?", "It Started How?" and "Is It Done Yet?" we introduce strategies we've developed to teach transitions, leads, and conclusions, respectively. Our work has shown us that these strategies seem to fall along a continuum, from easily applied to more challenging. Although we present these strategies in the "Revising and Assessing" section of this book, it's important to note that we introduce them informally from the start of the research process. Most of the emphasis on them comes, however, when students have a draft and begin to revise it.

Chapter 7, "Did We Succeed?" focuses on the assessment of research reports. In this chapter we provide examples of the tools we've designed to assess researching and reporting. Some of Barbara's fifth graders helped create these tools, and used most of them, as well. In addition, we take a close look at how states around the country are assessing writing performance. We try to dispel the myth that in order to achieve high scores on a standardized test, students must put aside what they know about good writing. Documentation from state reports, rubrics that evaluate writing in different states, and annotations that accompany student writing samples on standardized tests all support our premise to encourage students to go beyond the "safe" responses that follow specific, mind-numbing patterns of writing.

Each chapter in *Knowing How* contains "Teacher to Teacher" sections, in which we present instructional tips (what worked, why it worked, what to avoid). In addition, each chapter in Part 2 contains samples of student writing.

We will follow one fifth grader, Nick, through this entire process. Nick is a composite of many students. We'll watch how he formulates his research question about pandas, how he creates a data chart around a specific text structure, how he takes the data he collected and organizes them in a first draft, and how he applies various lead, transition, and conclusion strategies when revising his report.

In the appendixes you'll find a book report from a fourth grader, a science report from a fifth grader, and a persuasive essay from a seventh grader. In addition, there are tips for using technology, a list of nonfiction picture books, which could be used with upper elementary and middle school students to model the strategies found in Chapters 4, 5, and 6, and a list of all the strategies we discuss.

Our goal for this book is twofold: to describe what we learned about researching and nonfiction writing and to encourage you to extend the ideas and strategies found in this book—one step at a time. Once we demystify the process of researching and writing nonfiction, writers will know how to craft expository pieces that convey important information in engaging ways. What could be more rewarding than to see students push themselves to new levels by integrating these strategies into their expository writing? By helping students make their writing come alive, we are giving them the expertise to develop and craft all their writing for the future.

Acknowledgments

The students in Barbara Siegel's fifth-grade classes over the past three years have helped us learn a great deal about informational researching and report writing. They generously shared their insights and allowed us to test out practices with them. We are extremely grateful for all they've done for us and for all the assistance we've received from their parents. We also appreciate the support personnel who worked with Barbara's students. They have been wonderful to work with.

Without the help and support of several dedicated teachers who work in public and private schools in the Boston area, it would not have been possible to write this book. We'd like to thank Heather Carroll, Doris Claypool, Martha Fox, Rayna Tulysewski, and Lynda Verity for willingly taking time to try out some of our ideas with their students.

We'd also like to thank Suenita Lawrence for her assistance, Sheryl Saunders for sharing her knowledge about children's books, and Denise Marchionda for her invaluable feedback and encouragement.

Researching

Everyone does research. Whether a middle school student checking out portable CD players, a high school junior looking at college choices, or an adult in need of a new car, we explore possibilities and make inquiries before making a decision. In most cases, we talk to others and share ideas as we collect information. Often, we have a vague understanding of where we're headed when we begin, but it's not until we've spent some time gathering information that we can begin to focus our inquiry around one main point.

Let's pretend we're with Tayna's friends and see how she goes through this process. Tayna is a sixth grader who is in the market for a new portable CD player. She starts by talking to friends who own CD players and as she does so, she gradually picks up some of the relevant terminology: anti-shock, play time, digital play counter, and so on. All the while, she's beginning to differentiate between features that will be important for her to consider when purchasing this item and those that she knows she'll never use.

She checks out the ads in her local newspaper and slowly begins to narrow down her search. Because of the preliminary work she's done, she is in a better position to confront sales persons. She knows that she needs to find the product that will give her the best quality for the amount of money she can spend. This is what's driving this entire quest. She already has some information on which she'll continue to build.

Tayna realizes that it's time for her to get specific information. She wants to focus just on the following four factors in making her decision: cost, quality of sound, skip control, and headphones.

We head to the mall with Tayna and her friends with a defined purpose in mind: to compare different products with these features. Tayna's friends tease her about how prepared she is as she organizes the information she's collecting in a little chart she's made. We know, however, that having the notes will make it much easier for Tayna to make sense of the information when she gets back to her house. Next, Tayna analyzes the data she's collected and draws some conclusions. Tayna's done a thorough job of investigating the products and is ready to use her baby-sitting money to buy herself the CD player that she knows will be just right for her.

Like most researchers, Tayna had a big question that drove this process. She wanted to find the product that would suit her specific needs and budget considerations. What do you think the big question may be for the high school junior looking at college? Maybe she wants to know which college has a campus that would be comfortable and welcoming of her? The adult in need of a new car may wonder, "Is it financially better for me to buy a new car or lease one for a few years?" Smaller questions are subsumed within these bigger questions, but the bigger questions are needed to frame the research.

Very few people begin their research process by collecting random facts and then making connections to link the disparate facts together; yet, we sometimes ask students to do this when they encounter research projects in school. For example, fourth graders may be asked to research a state. They begin, not with a question that drives the exploration, but with a list of items to find: the state flower, its population, famous people from the state, the state capital, and so forth. They end up with interesting facts, but they can't easily write a cohesive report or draw conclusions that lead them somewhere. It may be better to begin such an investigation with a big question like "How does California's location along the Pacific Ocean affect its economy?" To answer this, students would come across many smaller pieces of information, and, in addition, they would end up with a body of knowledge that they could transfer to other situations.

Researching takes time. It's hard work. It can get messy and the process is often nonlinear. Our goal in Part 1 of this book is to acknowledge that researching is a complex process. It should be driven by our curiosity and by our need to understand the world in which we live.

In the first part of *Knowing How: Researching and Writing Nonfiction 3–8,* we focus on how to help students select a topic, design a research question, collect data in a structured way, and organize them to compose a first draft of a research paper. As you read along, we hope you'll keep in mind the out-of-school research you've done recently, whether it is related to renting an apartment, buying a new appliance, planning a vacation, or maybe just finding a new recipe. You may want to ask yourself why you conducted the research, what processes you used to collect and organize information, and how you used the information you gathered. Everyone does research. Knowing how to make it meaningful for our students and educationally sound is a challenge that many of us face. In the next three chapters, we'll describe how we've been attempting to meet this challenge.

Getting There from Here

*We do research to answer our own questions, and we write up
research to answer the questions for others.*
—Karen Tracey, *Teaching Freshmen to Understand
Research as a Process of Inquiry*

It's not easy to research a topic and write an informational report. Nick, a fifth grader, can attest to that. He has been researching pandas for several weeks and finished his final draft last night. It's due today. In class, his teacher asks for volunteers to read their reports out loud and Nick volunteers. He stands tall and begins:

The Panda Bear

I am doing a report on the panda bear. I picked the panda bear because it is cute and cuddly. I hope you enjoy my report and learning about this animal.

The panda bear lives only in western China. It lives in China because that is where its food is. It mainly eats bamboo and that's where it is grown. It has a black patch over both eyes. There is also black across its shoulders. The males are larger than the females. The males can weigh up to 220 pounds while the female is around 180 pounds.

Pandas live alone most of the time. They mate in the Spring. It takes about 3 to 6 months for the baby to be born. If two cubs are born then only one survives. The baby is only about 3 to 5 ounces and depends alot on its mother to survive.

Unlike other bears pandas do not hibernate. They don't have a permanent den but in the winter they live in dens or hollow trees.

The panda is endangered. There are only about 1,500 in the wild. There are many worldwide groups to help save the panda. I hope they do.

I hope you liked my report. If you want to find out more about panda bears you can go to the library.

The End

Taking a Closer Look

As stated earlier, Nick is a composite of many students we've worked with throughout the years. We created Nick so that we could critique the strengths and weaknesses of his work, something we would never do in this forum with the writing samples of a real student.

If you were Nick's teacher, how would you evaluate his report? Let's begin with the title. Did it beg you to read on? Probably not. What about the body of the report? It's true that it is full of interesting facts, but the reader does not come away with a sense that Nick has learned anything substantive about panda bears. He probably paraphrased information from one resource, because if he used several sources, he may have found that scientists don't all agree that pandas are bears; some think they are related to raccoons! None of Nick's ideas gets developed, and the writing jumps around. He begins by talking about where pandas live. After that, he describes what they look like. Next, he points out some information about their babies. Then he mentions that they do not hibernate and that they are endangered. The paragraphs could have come in any order. They are not connected in any way. What about Nick's conclusion? He ends the report by sending the reader to the library for more information. If we were evaluating this report, we'd have to note that it is devoid of Nick's own voice, which adds to the piece's dull and uninviting tone.

Nick's teacher knows that she needs to help Nick with his researching and reporting, but where does she begin? Perhaps she needs to ask herself the following questions:

- How can I help Nick envision researching as an inquiry process in which he seeks out answers to a substantive question that is important to him?
- How do I ensure that he takes away from the experience a body of knowledge and skills that he can transfer to other learning situations?
- What can I do to help Nick improve the quality of his writing?
- How do I nudge him on so that his next experience with researching and reporting is more positive?

These are big questions. As you'll see in the next sections, we've been thinking about them for quite a while now.

The Way It Was

Several years ago, Mary, an associate professor at a local university, and Barbara, a fifth-grade teacher in a metropolitan school district, worked side by side to investigate student researching and report writing. A grant enabled Mary to spend about ninety minutes one day a week in Barbara's room. At that time, Barbara was thinking about revising the way she had been teaching report writing to her fifth graders. Inservice workshops and new professional books (Harvey 1998; Short et al. 1996) prompted Barbara to think about research as inquiry based—as a tool for having her students design question-driven projects as opposed to fact-driven projects.

In prior years, Barbara spent six to eight weeks each fall having her students complete animal research reports. The students began by writing questions (which were usually literal) about the animal they chose to research. Next, they turned the questions into topics. For example, Where does the animal live? was related to Habitats; What does the animal eat? was related to Survival. They completed outlines (tables of contents) based on the topics (categories) they created. Before students began to collect data, they were taught note-taking skills. Once they collected and sorted the information, the students wrote their first drafts, which followed their outlines. Prior to completing a final draft, they revised their work and, in some cases, collected more data. Technology, such as the computer and Internet, was used throughout this process.

We both agree that this popular model, similar to the one proposed by Rief (1999), is valuable for many reasons. It gave learners in Barbara's class a structured format for collecting data. In addition, since everyone had similar questions about their animals, appropriate resources could be made available. Finally, this method enabled us to teach students how to break down a research topic into smaller, manageable pieces; how to organize their time and data; and how to structure a report using the categories and subcategories from the table of contents as distinct paragraphs in the report. However, current research and our experiences have shown us that a different type of learning may result when researchers are engaged in an inquiry-based approach to information reporting.

Dispelling Prevalent Myths

Before we go into detail about the research-and-writing process we've been using for the past several years, it may be beneficial to consider three myths that we had to address before we could move ahead in our thinking. Challenging these myths helped us get from where we were a few years ago to where we currently stand in our development. After listing these three myths, we'll address each one in more detail.

The first was related to the large issue of classroom environment. We believed that careful attention to the pedagogical setting in which researching was taught related only marginally to the anticipated outcomes. The second myth we dispelled related to a slightly narrower issue—one's disposition toward researching and reporting. We believed that report writing was a straightforward process of gleaning facts, organizing them, and reporting out what was learned. The third myth focused on the nitty-gritty of reporting. It dealt with how much time we devoted to each part of the researching process. We identified with other teachers who believed that researching the topic should consume most of the students' time in this process, whereas selecting the topic could be completed rather quickly. The emphasis was on gathering information.

Let's look at each of these myths, the information that helped us dispel each one, and how our practices have changed.

Myth No. 1

The pedagogical setting in which researching is taught relates only marginally to the anticipated outcomes.

It always made sense to us to believe it was appropriate to use a process approach for most forms of writing, but it was a different story (no pun intended) when it came to researching and report writing. When introducing or reinforcing these skills, we believed it was important to direct the students through the pieces of this task. The teacher made all the decisions. This was the model we grew up using and, not surprisingly, we continued to create this type of pedagogical setting for researching as novice and not-so-novice teachers. The teacher designed the task, determined what needed to be taught, and provided all feedback to the students. New information and changing instructional practices, however, have demonstrated that there are other, perhaps more effective ways to teach informational reporting.

What Information Helped Us Challenge This Myth?

Over the past few years, we've redefined our view about the roles that teachers and students play in constructing meaning. The introduction of the writing process, the implementation of writer's workshop, the whole language movement, and the impact of the inquiry cycle have played an enormous role in how we now manage the dailiness of our classes. Our students take a much more active part in the meaning-making process than ever before. According to Bergin and LaFave (1998), who conducted important research on motivation, the following eight considerations are central to this way of teaching and learning:

- choice
- personal goals for students

- assessment that focuses on "competencies" rather than "failures"
- experiences that lead to success
- modeling
- social engagement
- an environment that is emotionally encouraging and that fosters risk taking
- learning experiences that are self-motivating (p. 321)

How Did This Information Inform Our Practice?
What Did We Change?

Our changing view of how children construct meaning is reflected in many aspects of the classroom environment and in our teaching practices. As you walk into Barbara's fifth-grade classroom, you'll notice that the desks are arranged in sets of four or five to encourage collaborative exchanges. In the middle of the room you'll see a round table, which serves as a meeting place where all twenty-five students can gather together in close proximity to view demonstrations or to look at materials. It's not uncommon to find two or three children sitting together at a computer or planning something in a corner of the room.

We recognize that learning is a social process, but within this setting each of Barbara's fifth graders quickly understands that he has a responsibility to contribute to classroom activities on a regular basis. No one can sit back and be passive. Barbara often says, "Raise your hand if you haven't had a chance to share your ideas yet" or "Iris, we haven't heard from you in a while, what have you been thinking?" Students now participate in some of the assessment practices we rely on and often contribute to the design of these tools. Conferencing, group sharing, rubrics, and written teacher feedback are used for formative (ongoing) and summative (culminating) assessments and evaluations.

Along with taking some responsibility for their own learning, students need to feel comfortable taking risks. Time is given at the start of each research project for students to explore potential topics and materials. It's during this phase, before they commit to a specific research question, that they evaluate the resources that are available to them. All students are expected to find material that is appropriate for their level of development. They are encouraged to select their own research topics and try out different strategies while writing and revising their reports (see Part 2 for descriptions of the writing strategies we've developed and introduced).

As we noted at the beginning of this chapter, content-area researching and reporting are not easy. They are complex tasks that involve reading, writing, and a great deal of thinking. We're not suggesting that the classroom environment we've established promotes learning experiences that are self-motivating for all learners. We have found, however, that learners in general do seem to be more excited about researching when we deliberately consider the eight factors that Bergin and LaFave (1998) believe enhance pedagogical settings.

Myth No. 2

Report writing is a straightforward process of gleaning facts, organizing them, and reporting out what was learned.

Since all of us are familiar with the components of the research project, we can be lured into believing that it's a rather straightforward task. Students decide on a topic, collect information on note cards, prepare a bibliography, organize the information, and write the paper. On the surface, it doesn't seem all that complicated. This may be especially true if students already know how to take notes, know how to document sources for the bibliography, and have written reports in the past.

We may assign a topic—as Barbara did with her animal projects—and then teach students skills they need along the way. Oftentimes, however, we are discouraged when we receive the final papers. Like Nick's, they often are disorganized and appear to be a collection of underdeveloped, disparate pieces of information. Lane (1993) points out, "A skilled magazine writer can make any subject fascinating, yet in school we teach children to write research papers that often end up being lists of facts nailed together instead of a legitimate inquiry into a topic" (p. 18). Most disturbing, they may not demonstrate that the student has claimed ownership of the new information. Part of the problem may stem from an underlying assumption that the steps in this process are not difficult. Perhaps, however, there is much more to this process than we have been led to believe.

What Information Helped Us Challenge This Myth?

One factor that plays a key role in how students approach the research project is the stance they take toward the assignment; in other words, how the student views the task. Many students (and maybe teachers) see the task as one of finding and organizing information. Nelson and Hayes (1988) describe this type of process as "content-driven." Barbara, and perhaps most of us, used this model for years. When taking a content-driven stance, students locate, collect, and organize information that fits nicely into previously determined headings and subheadings (or categories). These predetermined headings form the structure of the report. Each heading becomes a new paragraph or section. When each heading or subheading contains enough information, the report is complete. We remember using this model all through school. We hunted for facts, used many sources so our teachers would know we spent time at the library, and neatly arranged all the index cards into piles on our desk. In some cases, we didn't even understand what we had copied, but it sounded impressive and it fit into a category, so we felt fortunate and used it. Writing the report was the easy part. We just had to connect the ideas on the cards into paragraphs. We mastered this process over time, but the information we collected—the facts—never became ours.

As a student, Mary loved to include lots of direct quotes in her reports. There were several legitimate reasons for doing this: first, she was sure they would impress the teacher, who would know that she worked hard hunting for information. Second, the original words of published authors always sounded better than her own words, so why take time trying to improve them? Third, good reports contained lots of quotes—at least that's what she believed at the time.

Both of us have used this framework with countless numbers of students in the past. It is the paradigm that we learned, and it has been the paradigm in schools around the country for many years. With new research, however, this approach to teaching researching and report writing may be changing.

Rather than relying on a "content-driven" perspective, Nelson and Hayes (1988) suggest that we encourage students to approach the task from an "issue-driven" stance. From this perspective, students investigate an issue or pose a question that eventually leads them to a thesis statement. They then analyze and shape ideas relevant to the thesis into something that is meaningful to them. It is this transformation of ideas—how they manipulate and synthesize information—that causes students to think critically, to draw conclusions, and to assimilate new information into their existing schema.

When assigning research projects, it is easy to lose sight of the levels of thinking that we need to draw on in order to "write from sources" (Hayes et al. 1992). McGregor (1994) found that "all levels of Bloom's taxonomy [knowledge, comprehension, application, analysis, synthesis, and evaluation] were continually required" (p. 129). She determined that students primarily use the "knowledge level" during the "pre-focus exploration" stage, when they are activating prior knowledge and adding on to their existing body of knowledge. Higher levels of thinking were evident throughout the process, especially during the writing phase.

We've found from our experiences that we sometimes took the writing stage for granted. All the "hard" work was done by then. In the last stage of reporting, students merely put the pieces together. This may be truer when writing a report from a content-driven perspective, but it is definitely not the case when students report from an issue-driven stance. Spivey (1985) acknowledges that "discourse synthesis" requires writers to take data from multiple sources, analyze them, reorganize them into organizational structures that differ from those found in the original sources, and make connections to integrate the new data. It's not surprising that our students have had a difficult time with the writing, perhaps because it does require so much higher-level thinking.

How Did This Information Inform Our Practice?
What Did We Change?

Many of the fifth graders in Barbara's class were already familiar with the content-driven model of reporting. Our challenge was to teach them how to approach this task from an issue-driven perspective, beginning with an issue, thesis statement, or question they wanted to investigate. Since neither of us had ever attempted informational reporting from this stance, we decided to engage in the process along with the students. We wanted to model exactly what we were doing and to discuss what we were experiencing from start to finish. We needed to understand firsthand how the process worked: where we would hit roadblocks, why one part of the process might be more complex than other parts, what emotions we were feeling and how they affected our progress. In the end, we wanted to know how the issue-driven stance differed from the content-driven stance and, more important, whether the issue-driven perspective enhanced learning in ways that the content-driven perspective hadn't in the past.

At this point, we felt comfortable with the theoretical underpinnings of the process, but we knew we would not be successful with this new approach unless we structured our time carefully, which brings us to our third myth.

Myth No. 3

Selecting a topic requires a fairly short amount of time. Researching the topic consumes most of the students' time.

Kuhlthau (1994) noted that the task of selecting a topic is often seen as "a preliminary act in preparation for the 'real' work ahead, rather than as a vital stage within the research process itself" (p. 30). Many of us have probably had the same experience that Short et al. describe in *Learning Together Through Inquiry* (1996). These teachers wanted students to decide on a topic or a research question quickly so they could get started "doing research." Unfortunately, they found, as we have, that when students jump into the data collection stage of reporting too soon, they tend to structure their reports around a collection of loosely related facts or around "superficial" questions, such as the one Iris, a fifth grader, originally wanted to use for her report: "How fast does the jaguar run?" When researchers base their reports on a series of literal questions, the report is often a series of disparate facts. Unless the researcher begins with a "big" question or a thesis statement, there is no uniting theme that binds the report together.

What Information Helped Us Challenge This Myth?

Many students believe that finding a topic is (or at least should be) effortless. We remember thinking this all the way from elementary school through graduate school. Each time we were given a research project to complete we ran an endless array of topics through our heads to find the right one. We worried that the teacher would expect us to have a topic selected by the next time we met, and that if we didn't, we'd have to explain why. We lost sleep suspecting that everyone else would be ahead of us. They'd be ready to start their library search and we'd be floundering around, wasting precious time. In our panic to begin, we sometimes selected a topic that was not a good match for us. It may have been too broad, too narrow, or too cognitively challenging. We can recall spending weeks researching topics that we weren't even interested in, just to be done with them. Our lack of passion and commitment sometimes stemmed from our lack of interest in the topic. We didn't own it. It probably never occurred to us that we needed to invest as much effort in shaping our topic as we put in to researching it. In the end, we seldom remembered the information we wrote about, perhaps because it's difficult to retain isolated facts in one's long-term memory or because we copied chunks of information from reference sources and never clearly understood what we were reading. Regrettably, we've probably all had similar experiences.

An ideal topic doesn't generally jump into one's head. In reality, worthwhile topics are formed, not found (Burdick 1997; Kuhlthau 1994). Kuhlthau (1994) broke down the research process into six steps: "receiving an assignment; selecting a topic; looking for a possible focus; forming a focus; gathering information and refining the focus; and writing the paper" (pp. 23–24). Notice how much time is spent in pre-data collecting. Four steps precede the start of the data collection. Gathering information for the report is the second-to-last step. Kuhlthau allows a considerable amount of time for reading, building background knowledge, thinking, and discovering. In addition, her work recognizes that emotional responses can accompany each stage of this process. According to Kuhlthau (1988, 1994), when the assignment is given, students often feel a sense of "uncertainty." They then move to a feeling of "optimism" when they select a topic. "Confusion" is commonly associated with the stage in which students look for a possible focus. When they form a focus, they may feel relieved that they now have found some clarity. Gathering information and refining the focus generally leads students to feel that they now have a "sense of direction." They may feel "confident." Finally, when the paper is complete, students feel either "satisfied or concerned that something is missing" (p. 25). We're not sure all students feel these same emotions as they go through the process, but Kuhlthau's work helped us realize the need to slow down the process and to understand that both cognitive and affective factors need consideration when we engage in informational researching. Formulating a thoughtful, focused question is not easy. Short et al. (1996) recommend that students "muck around" and spend time "wandering and wondering" (p. 162), especially when they begin to explore various research options.

It's often difficult to find the necessary time to let learners "muck around." There seems to be so much to cover in today's curriculum and so little time. Moreover, some of us may neglect to allow enough time for students to generate questions because we may not realize how difficult this is for them (Tower 2000). This may be particularly true for students who have had little experience generating substantive questions. Students typically answer questions; they don't create them. Most students are probably unaware that there are different categories of questions (literal, interpretive, evaluative, and so on) unless they have been exposed to such strategies as Question the Author (Beck et al. 1997) or Raphael's (1986) Question-Answer Relationship (QAR).

How Did This Information Inform Our Practice? What Did We Change?

The two of us and Barbara's fifth graders all began at the same point. Instead of jumping right into the data-collection process, we began our first attempt at using the issue-driven model by taking time to consider several topics, to explore available resources, and to build background knowledge. Barbara decided to research the Tasmanian devil. Mary decided to research raccoons. Each of us had a personal interest in the animal we chose. Barbara and her husband have long been fans of the Tasmanian devil. Barbara wanted to learn more about the real animals on which the famous cartoon is based. Mary's daughter, at that time, was nervous about walking down her driveway at night because raccoons lived in the surrounding trees. Mary wanted information about raccoons to appease her daughter's fears. We shared our reasons for selecting these animals with the fifth graders and encouraged them to investigate animals that were important to them.

The time we had to explore possible topics provided us with an opportunity to see whether or not we wanted to learn more about the animals we chose. We knew this was a preliminary search and that we were not committed to any topic at this point. Our initial browsing confirmed for us that we wanted to learn more about the Tasmanian devil and raccoons. We could decide after our initial exploration, however, whether these topics were appropriate. If not, we could have chosen a different animal to investigate. This was the case for some of the fifth graders. Kevin, for example, was interested in snakes at first but was unable to find sufficient information about any one snake. The more he looked, the less interested he became in researching them. Nevertheless, while exploring snakes, he came across some information on African elephants that really piqued his interest. During a conference with Kevin, we encouraged him to switch topics. Harvey (1998) noted that our "passion"—our interests, what we get excited about—should "be at the heart of inquiry" (p. 12). We couldn't agree more.

☑ Checking In with Nick

We began this chapter with a look at Nick's panda report. Let's jump ahead and take a look at the report Nick turned in at the end of the project.

Although there is still room for improvement, the revised report revolves around one two-part question: Why are there so few pandas left in the world and what can we do to protect them? This one controlling idea helped Nick add depth to his report. It also eliminated the temptation to copy chunks of disparate information from an encyclopedia or other resource.

Certain to Survive?

It's [sic] newborn body weighs only 2 oz., but eventually it will eat about 30 pounds of food each day. Who could eat this much food? An African elephant? A Great White Shark? Nope. The one with the big appetite is the cuddly panda.

You may be wondering where they get all this food. Actually, they eat mostly bamboo, which can be found only in southwest China. It's sad to say that only about 1,000 of them live in the wild and another 100 live in zoos around the world. Why are there so few and what are people doing to protect them?

A long time ago, hunters killed pandas for their fur. It was used for rugs. The pandas had thick fur that kept them warm in their cold weather.

When Pandas were first discovered, they were killed so scientists could study their skin and bones. They were trying to learn more about them. They knew they looked sort of like bears but they didn't hibernate like bears and they can't walk on their hind legs. Also, pandas can grab onto bamboo easily because one of their bones in their wrists is larger and longer than the others. They also have strong jaws and strong teeth witch helps them eat the hard bamboo. If you was a scientist wouldn't you want to find out about all these unique things about pandas too?

Another reason there are so few pandas is because people have built homes and farms in the mountain valleys of China where pandas used to live. The pandas had to move up into the colder mountains to get food and water. This was not good because they ran out of their food supply and because they had to live closer to men who could kill them.

Today the Chinese government is protecting pandas and their land. It's now against the law to kill them and officials plant bamboo so pandas always have enough food.

Although man has killed lots of pandas in the past now people everywhere want to help pandas. Pandas have been brought to zoos where zookeepers give them vitamins and put them on special diets to keep them healthy. Sometimes they live in dark, air-conditioned sections of the zoo, so they feel like they are at home in the mountains of China. Pandas like to be near water, so zookeepers make sure they have plenty to use for drinking, playing and cooling off. Pandas who live in the wild usually live about 15 years. Pandas who live in captivity can live into their 20s.

No matter if the pandas live in China or in a zoo, it seems that everyone is now working hard to make sure they live long, safe lives. Perhaps this will help keep pandas from becoming extinct so people in years to come can also enjoy these cuddly-looking animals.

Nick's paper is now focused and has a strong voice. The report now has an intriguing title, which is likely to raise questions for the reader. The lead grabs the reader's attention. The transitions enable the reader to follow Nick's logical train of thought. Nick ends the paper by drawing a conclusion and looking to the future. This conclusion pulls the pieces together. Equally important, Nick has demonstrated an understanding of the giant panda's plight. The possibility of extinction that pandas face is an issue for other animals in the world as well. Nick can now take his knowledge of the giant panda and transfer it to other endangered animals. He has a knowledge base that cuts across topics. He can use it to draw conclusions and think about larger issues that impact other animals. This is something he may not have been able to do with a compilation of loosely related facts that may have surfaced from a content-driven report. We think Nick has accomplished a great deal. As Tracey (1997) aptly points out, "We do not undertake research to demonstrate to our teachers our ability to amass long bibliographies and summarize, paraphrase, and quote from them, but rather, we undertake research to answer questions that matter to us and to our readers" (p. 3).

What's Next?

From the information highlighted in this chapter we designed a research model that has proven effective for us. The remainder of the book will delve into the following components of the process:

Stage 1: Exploring Topics
Stage 2: Knowing What You Know (and Don't Know)
Stage 3: Formulating a Research Question
Stage 4: Designing a Framework for Collecting Data
Stage 5: Narrowing the Search
Stage 6: Recording and Organizing Relevant Data
Stage 7: Going from Data to First Draft
Stage 8: Revising Draft(s)
Stage 9: Presentation

We will be coming back to Nick's work in each chapter to demonstrate how he grows as a researcher and writer. Although Nick is a figment of our imagination, all other writing samples included in this book reflect the work of real upper elementary and middle school students.

Journeying from Topic to Research Question

Jennifer was a precocious four-year-old who asked questions incessantly. As a teenager, Mary would baby-sit for her once in a while when her parents went out for an evening. Mary recalls sitting beside Jennifer on a sofa late one winter night. While looking out her living room window into the dark neighborhood street, Jennifer began, "I wonder where the trees go at night?" Mary looked at her, thinking she was probably kidding, but she was dead serious. At the time, Mary didn't appreciate Jennifer's constant need for information. In fact, her questions drove Mary to distraction. She was unaware of how hard this little girl was working to make sense of her world. Now the real-world questions and issues that consume young learners fascinate her.

Even young children like Jennifer have the ability to generate "big," important questions. We witness this all the time when we're with children. As they watch the evening news they wonder why a shark bit a boy's arm off in knee-deep water when sharks don't normally come close to shore and don't usually attack humans. During a powerful summer storm they question what causes the lightning. On a bike ride around the neighborhood, they notice an electric car in a nearby driveway. On the side of the car, in large, green, block lettering the words "ELECTRIC VEHICLE" stand out against the white paint. The car seems to be attached to a long extension cord that's always connected to an outlet on the side of the house. They speculate, "Is the electric car better than a car that runs on gas?"

There are no easy answers to these questions. To respond to the last one, for example, we would need to think about environmental issues (How do the fuel emissions of the electric car compare to those of gas cars?), cost factors (How expensive is it to buy? to maintain? to run?), and convenience (How often does it need to be recharged? How far can it go at one time? How fast can it go?). The little questions are necessary. They relate directly to the bigger one. The little ones may remain disparate and unfocused, however, unless we start with the bigger question. The bigger question leads us to a conclusion, whereas a series of disjointed little questions can't.

Before the Beginning

Prior to starting research projects, it may be wise to consider setting up some structures to help ensure success.

At-Home Support

Barbara begins the year by letting parents know how essential their support is for this research project. She introduces it at the open house, which is held on Curriculum Night, and follows up by sending a letter home to parents (see Figure 2.1). She insists that the letter (and all other communication) be signed by a parent/guardian so she knows it has been received. You'll notice that she lets parents know that the research process will be divided into two parts: researching and writing. In this letter, however, she includes information only about Part 1 so they don't get overwhelmed.

In the letter, Barbara explains exactly what she will do in this research project: approve research topics; help students design data charts; work with them to locate and evaluate appropriate resources; teach them how to take notes; and provide them with strategies to use for leads, transitions, and conclusions. She reminds parents that they can help by monitoring what their children do and by ensuring that the fifth graders spend thirty minutes each evening working on this project. She also lets parents know that if they are unable to assist their children, the students can work on their research at a designated time after school with her or with support personnel. She includes in the letter a timetable and two copies of a calendar that presents the same information in a different format (see Figure 2.2). One copy of the calendar stays at home, hopefully where it's clearly visible, and the second copy goes into each student's working folder. Barbara attaches a sheet of paper to this letter. On it, there is a place for parents to sign, indicating that they have read the letter. Parents are invited to use the remainder of the paper to write down their comments or questions.

In-School Support

One major goal for our research projects has always been to help students learn new organizational skills. It's important for each student to have a battery of accessible strategies, to know which strategies are effective for him, and when to use them. Like most teachers, we painstakingly teach students

Figure 2.1 Barbara's Letter Home to Parents

(handwritten at top right: —too long! —short + sweet)

September 17, 2001

Dear Parents,

As we discussed at Curriculum Night, the students will be undertaking an extensive inquiry-based research project ending around the December recess. Their objective will be to investigate a type of open-ended question about a topic in which they are interested. This "big" question will encourage students to develop their higher-level thinking skills and urge them to analyze data they find. In order to develop their questions, they will first need to acquire some background information. For this reason, I would appreciate having each student acquire books and other materials related to a subject of interest to him/her no later than Monday, September 24. I would like students to read this material for a minimum of thirty minutes daily. This assignment may take the place of having students read independently for thirty minutes nightly. I appreciate your support in this matter.

This project will have two components: a research phase and a writing phase. After I approve their research topics, I will collaborate with students to design data charts—a way for them to organize their note taking. I will also work with them on how to take notes and how to find and judge relevant information. Concurrently, I will help students develop strategies to locate information on the Internet and to examine the reliability of these sources. During this time, I'll be exposing students to nonfiction writing through daily read-aloud of picture books and other expository texts. In Part 2, the writing/revision stage, students will turn their notes into a report that focuses on the research question and is written in their own voice. Reports will not sound like and parrot encyclopedia articles. During this process, I will teach strategies for transitions and leads so that students will be able to express themselves coherently in a more exciting approach.

Since this process is complex, I am only going to present guidelines for Part 1 in this letter. When we are ready to begin Part 2, I will send out information for the writing/revision stage. Enclosed, at this time, are two calendars: one that is to be kept at home for your reference and the other that we will put into a student research folder. Below is another look at this timetable:

Part 1: The Research Phase

Monday, September 24–Tuesday, October 9: Background Reading

Wednesday, October 10–Monday, October 15: Topic Development

October 16–19: Outdoor Education (Science Camp)—no work on project

Monday, October 22: Data Chart Design

Tuesday, October 23–Tuesday, November 6: Research and Note Taking

Again, I am most grateful for your support in monitoring your child's work. I want your children to spend at least thirty minutes each night on each aspect of Part 1. If you would like, your child is welcome to stay after school from 2:15–2:45 P.M. on Mondays, Wednesdays, and Thursdays to work with me. Please do not hesitate to contact me at any time with any questions or concerns.

Sincerely,

Barbara Siegel

- -

I have seen the letter about the inquiry-based research project.

_____

Parent Signature

Comments:

Figure 2.2 Calendar for the Research Phase of the Researching and Reporting Process

Sunday	Monday	Tuesday	Wednesday	Thursday	Friday	Saturday
September	24 Begin Background Reading	25	26	27	28	29
30	October 1	2	3	4	5	6
7	8	9 End Background Reading	10 Begin Topic Development	11	12	13
14 (Science Camp from Tuesday, October 16, through Friday, October 19—no work on project)	15 End Topic Development 22 Data Chart Design	23 Begin Research and Note Taking	24	25	26	27
28	29	30	31	November 1	2	3
4	5	6 End Research Phase				

how to budget their time, organize all the necessary materials for informational researching, and monitor their progress.

To help students get organized, Barbara gives each student two different-colored folders with pockets: a working folder and a reference folder. → *finished*
Initially, they begin with just a working folder. During the research phase, they store time lines of due dates, their calendars, photocopies of articles they've saved, and Internet information they've downloaded, along with note cards, data charts, and any other pertinent research material. Students keep these materials organized in their working folder so they can refer to them when they write their first draft. When they finish their first draft, they then transfer these research materials to a pocket in the reference folder. As Barbara introduces new strategies, they are held in the other side of the reference folder. From this time on, the working folder contains only the current drafts. As teachers well know, students may become overwhelmed with papers. The dual-folder system enables them to keep current, working documents in one place and organized reference materials in a separate, accessible place.

Ready to Begin

Parents and students know where we're headed and we have folders in place, so it's time to begin the research project! This is an undertaking that should not be done by one person alone, if possible. The classroom teacher should involve the support staff in the school such as the librarian, media specialist, Title I teachers, reading people, special needs personnel, ESL staff, assistant teachers, and student teachers. It is essential that everyone understands the goals of the project and your expectations. They must hear the messages and guidelines you give to all students. These people can prove immensely valuable throughout the research and writing processes.

As shown in Chapter 1, we've broken down the research and writing processes into nine stages, from exploring topics to presentations. Although we presented them in a linear fashion, these steps may overlap and students may move back and forth among them as needed. For example, a student may begin Stage 5, Narrowing the Search, and realize that she needs to modify her research question in light of the data she's found. In effect, she'll return temporarily to Stage 3, Formulating a Research Question. This recursive approach is fine, and should be encouraged If necessary. In this chapter we'll examine the first three stages: Exploring Topics, Knowing What You Know (and Don't Know), and Formulating a Research Question.

Stage 1: Exploring Topics

Unless the teacher assigns a specific, well-defined topic (e.g., the Underground Railroad), students face the task of looking for one. This process takes time. We generally give the students about two to three weeks to explore potential topics because, as we have stated, it's probably the single most significant part of a successful report. Barbara had spent years collecting appropriate materials and resources on animals, so we decided to pilot the "issue-driven" research model (Nelson and Hayes 1988) with animal reports. We also wanted to keep some of our prior tried-and-true practices in place as we began to implement new ones.

We expected students to use this exploration or browsing time to see what animals might interest them and what resources were available in and outside of school. Before we sent them off to explore possible topics, we gathered the fifth graders around Barbara's round table to brainstorm various places they could look. Our first experience doing this produced the following list:

science museums in the area (Museum of Science—Boston; Worcester
    Science Center)
two nearby zoos (Franklin Zoo and Stone Zoo)

a friend

the town library

web sites such as the National Wildlife Federation; Yahooligans; Jeeves
    for Kids

someone who works in the field

the Discovery Channel television shows such as *Animal Planet*

videos from the local library or video-rental stores

children's magazines such as *National Geographic World* and *Time for Kids*

encyclopedias—both hard copies and CD versions

pet stores

books from teachers they had in prior grades

audubon society

Moving Beyond Animal Research

We were impressed with the wide range of resources the students considered, and we could also see how much of an influence technology had in their lives outside of school. Time to explore gives students opportunities to decide on a topic that matches their interests and own level of development. They become more realistic about whether or not the topic is doable as they engage in more reading.

On September 24, they needed to bring to class some evidence that they had been exploring potential topics and narrowing their search. This initial check-in was about a week after the assignment was given. There was a range of responses to this task. One student came with seven resources, while three students didn't have any resources at all. During a whole-class exchange that afternoon, students discussed their progress and experiences. They let each other know what topics they were thinking about researching and what aspect of these broad topics they were interested in pursuing, if they had gotten this far in their thinking.

Kirk, a bright boy, noted that his original topic was "soccer." He soon realized, however, that he knew a great deal about this sport and what he hadn't yet learned was too abstract for him to figure out from books. He wanted to challenge himself, though, and decided to explore solar energy to see what resources he could find. On September 24, he had some resources, but he needed to continue to read in order to narrow his search. Kirk was excited about this new topic and eager to do more reading. Another student, Sondra, was interested in elephants, but again wasn't sure of exactly where she was headed with this topic. Barbara asked if she was planning to research a certain elephant: African, Asian . . . After thinking a moment, Sondra said, "Perhaps I'll compare and contrast African and Asian elephants." The next step for her was to find resources and see if this would be an appropriate topic for her research.

Jenn had been doing background reading on horses. She thought she would try to find out why people mount horses from the left. This is an interesting question, but maybe not one that would make a good research question for Jenn. During the discussion, someone asked Jenn if all horses are the same. She replied, "No, they are all different." The Title I teacher, who happened to be in the room at the time, picked up on this and asked if Clydesdales would make good racehorses? This question led the students to think about the body parts of different horses and what characteristics a racehorse may have. Jenn was going to continue to read about horses but now she had moved beyond her original line of thinking. The scope of her topic had broadened and her exploration led her to a new area to research.

It's important to take the time to check in with students, to hold these discussions, and to ask questions at this point in the process. Teachers can guide students to appropriate topics and different aspects of topics while they are still exploring various possibilities. Elizabeth, a girl in this class, was exploring figure skating. She found information about the history of figure skating and was amazed by it. Elizabeth, unlike Sondra, had to narrow down her topic. Other students in the class helped suggest possible areas to consider. Sometimes Barbara lets students know what former students have chosen as research questions, but she never gives students a question to research. Instead, she reminds them that there are all kinds of things to think about when researching a topic and that they need to find something that interests them.

If a student suggests a topic that you know is too difficult, it may be wise to let him proceed rather than discourage him at this point. If the student finds that the topic isn't suitable, you may be able to guide him to a more appropriate related topic.

You may have another student who is very capable but doesn't challenge himself. He may choose a topic with which he's very familiar. For example, Jimmy was completely taken with everything connected to the World Wrestling Federation (WWF). Every chance he got, he connected WWF to his schoolwork. He read WWF material during Drop Everything and Read (DEAR). The wrestlers made their way into every writing assignment. We knew exactly what he would research, if allowed to choose his own topic. What should the teacher do? There are several options: she could give him some topics and allow him to choose one from her list; she could let him research whatever he wanted as long as it wasn't WWF-related; she could allow him to research the WWF, knowing that the formation of the inquiry question would be crucial to what he gained from this researching experience. If we found ourselves in this position, we would opt for the third choice. Think of how much we all learn from visiting a museum more than once. Each time, we probably focus on something that we didn't notice on previous visits. The same holds true for students who have a strong interest in one area; there is always more to learn. The teacher needs to be the guide in helping her students come up with questions that are stimulating and challenging—questions that will help the student explore the topic in depth and not just rehash what is already known.

Some researchers find an appropriate topic early in the two-week period. Barbara knew right from the start that she wanted to research the Tasmanian devil. At home and school she had a collection of Taz items such as cups, T-shirts, mouse pads, and key chains. She was curious about what a real Tasmanian devil was like. She wondered why this animal was found in only one part of the world. She used the exploration time to see if she would be able to find appropriate resources.

Mary, on the other hand, didn't have a topic in mind when she began. She visited the children's room of the university library. She located the shelves that housed books about animals and began to consider the subject matter. She noticed that there were multiple books about some of the animals and made a mental note. Those were the animals she considered most strongly at the beginning because she knew there were appropriate resources available for her to use. Finding several resources on a few possible topics helped her limit her search for the time being, but at this stage, she was not restricting herself to just that group. After a few minutes of browsing, she was drawn to a cover photograph of an adorable raccoon and decided to concentrate on this animal, at least for the time being. She planned to share information she found with her daughter, who was fearful of these masked creatures.

It's important to emphasize that it was our personal interests and needs that led us to select the Tasmanian devil and the raccoon to research. Our students had similar experiences. Ariel investigated the Pomeranian because a friend owned one; Kathryn researched the polar bear because she thought they were cute; Chloe had a houseguest from Japan and wanted to know more about the country; Greg wanted to be an artist and decided to learn more about Picasso.

There is no one right way to find a topic. For some of us, an immediate interest or need led us directly to a topic. For others, the research topic slowly evolved. We considered options, eliminated possibilities, and gradually moved in a focused direction. What's important to remember, however, is that this was an active process for all of us. Nobody just sat back and waited for an idea to strike.

While exploring possible topics, students may or may not take notes. It's up to you and your students. During this part of the process, we generally don't have students take notes. We want them to tap into resources, to get a general overview of several possible topics, and to evaluate the availability of appropriate materials. Taking notes at this point may limit the range of possibilities that students investigate. Some students may get bogged down in the physical aspects of writing. They may feel committed to a topic and be reluctant to start again once they have written notes. In addition, taking notes at this point takes time away from exploring topics. This may cause students to settle on a topic prematurely just because they don't have enough time to explore *and* take notes on multiple topics. Note taking will come later, but for now we want students to keep their options somewhat open. The goal for each student is to narrow the search down just enough to find a topic that is of interest and is reasonable to investigate.

Stage 2: Knowing What You Know (and Don't Know)

Once students think they may have a probable topic (nothing is definite yet), whether after an hour or six days of examining possibilities, they should begin to think about what they know and what they want to find out (Ogle 1986). This is the second stage in the process for all students. Mary began to model what she was thinking by creating a simple T-chart on the chalkboard. She labeled the columns: What I Know and What I Want to Know. Beginning with the "What I Know" column, she recorded her thoughts and talked briefly about each one, noting if the information came from her own experiences or from her "browsing." The students were eager to help her add to the list. Although they had information to contribute, Barbara reminded them that this was Mary's T-chart. It should include just what she knows and what she wanted to know.

What I Know	What I Want to Know
Usually raccoons are out at night (nocturnal) unless sick	Where do they live?
Climb trees	How did they get their masks?
Eat from bird feeders and trash cans	What would an adult do in a typical day?
Have masks and stripes	How big do they get?
People shouldn't go near them	How long do they live?
Babies are called cubs	How do they help and hurt the environment?
	What enemies do they have?
	What behavior is okay and what would tell us if a raccoon has rabies?

We asked students to create T-charts for their research topics. It is much easier to brainstorm a list when researchers have spent time reading about their topic. That's why the preceding stage of the process is so essential. Next, we demonstrated how we used information from our T-charts to formulate our big research questions.

Stage 3: Formulating a Research Question

Modeling Our Process

We began by taking Mary's T-charts and explained that some of the questions under her "What I Want to Know" column were better research questions than others. Some of the questions were "little" questions: Where do they live? How big do they get? How long do they live? and perhaps What enemies do they have? We wanted to ask big questions, not little ones. We provided examples of big questions: What's being done to protect raccoons and people from rabies? How do raccoons defend against their enemies? Why do raccoons live in the places they do? Mary explained that she was going to research the good and bad things raccoons do for the environment. She recalled the incident with her daughter so the students would understand that she had a genuine interest in finding the answers to this question. She wasn't doing this research to collect facts. She was doing it to satisfy her own curiosity.

Neither of us anticipated the challenge we faced the first time we structured research projects around one substantive question. We didn't realize how difficult it would be for the fifth graders to distinguish between literal and open-ended questions. Barbara began by asking her fifth graders why they thought we were having them do research projects. The responses contained answers such as: to learn how to organize ideas, to learn facts, to learn how to gather information, to use sources, to raise our grades, and to get us ready for middle school. It was important at this point for them to understand exactly why we were involving them in this experience, so Barbara explained that the real reason for doing research is to find answers to the important questions we have. We stopped periodically throughout the research process to review and validate why we were approaching this task as we were. We included students in each of these discussions to ensure that the rationale was expressed in language they could understand. These short review sessions helped the students stay focused and monitor their own growth. Our discussions involved explaining the differences between different types of questions such as those that are factually based versus those that require higher-level thinking skills.

Since many of the students found it challenging to decide if questions were *big* or *little*, we asked them to think ahead and tell us what they might expect to find for an answer. If the question could be answered in a word or a few words, the question would be *little*. For example, "Where do they live?" could probably be answered in a few words: They live up in trees, in cities, in the woods, in the hollows of trees. This question would not lead to a report that was comprehensive and well developed. Jenn would have probably come to this conclusion, too, if she continued to research why people mount horses from the left. On the other hand, *big* questions, such as "How do the raccoon's physical appearance, his instincts, and survival skills help him stay alive?" would probably require a richer response and the use of several resources to answer completely.

We also pointed out one other category of questions—those that could not be answered. Take, for example, Why do raccoons have masks? This may be an interesting question, but not one that fifth graders could answer in a report. Knowing that not all questions have answers is another important part of learning how to conduct research.

Several students caught on to the difference between big and little questions after our initial discussions, but for many, this was still very abstract. Mary thought it might be interesting to use nonfiction picture books to model the process we use to formulate *big* research questions. Although Barbara was a bit hesitant at first—she wasn't sure that picture books had a place in fifth grade and was afraid the students would think they were too babyish—she was willing to take a risk and give it a try.

We selected books that were appropriate for her ten- to twelve-year-olds. We looked for books with illustrations that would hold the students' attention. In addition, the content had to appeal to upper elementary students. Mary believed that the conciseness of the writing would make it possible to complete an entire text in one period and still have time to provide a focused mini-lesson on big and little questions. Barbara, on the other hand, decided to slow down. She read only a few pages of a picture book each day and spent time engaging the students in thoughtful dialogues about the content. The students loved it. Two of the picture books Barbara used were *The Hindenburg* (O'Brien 2000) and *Eleanor* (Cooney 1996).

Using Picture Books to Formulate Big Questions

The Hindenburg explains in clear language what a dirigible is, how this aircraft was able to fly, and its impact on history. To illustrate the difference between big and little questions, Barbara explained that a little question might be, "How many people could ride in Count Zeppelin's dirigibles at one time?" O'Brien's book didn't tell us, but we could probably check a source or two and find the answer without too much trouble. But finding the answer to this question would not advance our understanding of the dirigible. In the long run, it would not matter if eight people or twenty-eight people could ride in it at once. It may be interesting to know the answer, but unless it is connected to other knowledge, it isn't all that relevant, and we probably would forget the answer over time.

Thinking up an open-ended, comprehensive question was more of a challenge. Barbara took advantage of some information that O'Brien included near the end of the book. He states that no one has been able to determine conclusively what caused the Hindenburg explosion. Some theorize that thunderstorms in the area produced static electricity, which ignited the hydrogen in the airship. Others wonder if a bomb may have caused it. Barbara explained that she was intrigued by this mystery. If this were her research project, she might try to find an answer to the following question: What was happening in 1937 that would cause people to question whether or not a bomb triggered the Hindenburg explosion on May 6?

In order to answer this question, she might research primary sources: newspaper stories from 1937, letters translated from German, photographs, information from the National Hydrogen Association, and so forth. Her research would probably focus primarily on social studies. Since the Nazis demanded that Eckener, the person who created the Hindenburg, place swastikas on the tail fins of the airship, Barbara would have to understand what was happening in Germany in the 1930s and what the Nazis represented. Those who suspect that a bomb was involved in the downing of the airship wonder whether the swastikas had anything to do with it. After Barbara collected data, she might write a persuasive essay to inform her readers of the historical context in which the Hindenburg existed.

Barbara could follow this same line of reasoning after reading *Eleanor* (Cooney 1996), a picture book that depicted the early life of Eleanor Roosevelt. This short biography concludes when Eleanor is still a teenager, but the afterword explains that she eventually marries Franklin Delano Roosevelt and becomes First Lady of the United States. A small, factual question might be, "How did she meet Franklin Delano Roosevelt?" A bigger, more significant question may be the one Barbara posed to her fifth graders, "How does someone who is so afraid and who comes from such a sad background become such a famous person?" This question requires a great deal of research. Students may have to learn about her personal life and about her accomplishments. This type of research may help some children think introspectively about ways in which they can affect their own destiny.

It is difficult for many students to see the subtle distinctions we try to make when discerning between big and little questions. Barbara has gone through this process of having her fifth graders formulate big questions for several years now. Along the way, she has saved examples of big and little questions from her former students to use as examples. Here are a few of their big questions:

> Do you ever wonder how figure skating and regular skating are alike and different? (Elizabeth)
> Are UFOs real or not? (Steve)
> Why has the white-tailed deer population been increasing over the years even though they are constantly being hunted for their buckskin? (Catherine)
> How did the universe start? (Kathryn, Armand)
> How do people train dolphins? (Jackie)
> What makes the Great Wall of China one of the Seven Wonders of the World? (Willy)

Doris, a colleague of ours, was going through this same process with her seventh graders. She was having them draft thesis statements rather than questions. These seventh graders were focusing on big ideas. Doris' students came up with the following ideas for their thesis statements:

Melanoma is one of the easiest types [of cancer] to battle. (Shawna)
In the Holocaust people died just because they were different. (Lisa)
Airbags should be optional in vehicles. (Ben)

Heather, a seventh-grade teacher, had students focus their research papers on causes and effects. Their topics included the causes that led to and the effects that followed from

The Costa Rican Migration Department for Refugees' (MDR) decision
    to grant 532 people refugee status in 2000 (Natalie)
Castro's revolution against Batista (Ethan)
Duvalier's leadership as Haiti's "President for Life." (Jenny)

Thinking up big questions and knowing the difference between them and little ones often takes time and practice. Barbara reinforced the idea of a big question by asking her students to transfer this understanding whenever they asked questions in other subject areas.

Teacher to Teacher

If you're working with younger students, you may want to spend more time modeling and reinforcing the concept of big and little questions. You would probably begin in a whole-group setting, move to smaller groups, then perhaps, spend time with individuals.

You may reinforce this concept by writing questions on index cards and asking small groups of students to sort them into big and little questions. They should be able to explain the rationale for their choices. Another way to provide practice in distinguishing between literal and open-ended questions may be to write questions on strips of paper and have the children help you tape them to the wall under the headings "Big Questions" and "Little Questions." Children can add to this list over the next several days or weeks.

Having the children always think ahead to what the possible answer(s) could be helped Barbara's students understand that a report based on a little question would only be a sentence or two long, whereas a report based on a big question could go on for pages. They knew that big questions often lead to memorable conclusions, whereas little questions often lead to a list of isolated facts.

From Data Charts to Big Questions

Once your students have a fairly solid understanding of how big and little questions differ, they should be ready to formulate their research questions. By this point in the process, each student should have her own T-chart ready. The next step is for each one to use information from the What I Want to Know column on her T-chart to formulate a big research question. Let's see how different students work through this process.

Andrew decided to investigate the arctic fox, an animal he had been interested in for some time. One question, taken directly from his chart, became his research question: How does the arctic fox survive in the arctic region?

What I Know	What I Want to Know
Lives in Arctic Its coat changes from season to season	What does it eat? How does it survive in the Arctic? What are its enemys [sic]? How do they treat their young? Do they burrow or live on surface?

For other students, deciding on their big question, or "hard" question as one fifth grader put it, involved combining and expanding some of the information from their charts. It wasn't as easy for them as it was for Mary and Andrew. Their big question wasn't in their What I Want to Know column. Take, for example, Nick's T-chart. As you recall from the last chapter, Nick is researching giant pandas. Nick's chart contained the following information:

What I Know	What I Want to Know
Live in China Eat bamboo Are endangered Do not hibernate (I think??) Some live in zoos Have white and black fur	How big are they when they are born? How long do they live? Besides bamboo, what else do they eat? How many giant pandas are there in the world? Is it hot or cold where they live in China?

Nick has quite a bit of information already, but he's unsure about what his big question should be. We may begin by asking him what he might expect to find as answers to the questions he has listed in the What I Want to Know column of his T-chart. Each question could probably be answered in a word or a couple of sentences; therefore, they would be little questions. We may be able to help Nick formulate a substantive question by combining and expanding on what he knows and/or wants to know.

He knows that giant pandas are endangered, and he'd like to know more about where and how they exist. Based on this, we may ask Nick questions that would lead him to a big question without giving him his research question directly. Since he wants to know how many giant pandas are in the world today, he probably has a hunch that there aren't too many pandas left. We might begin by asking him to explain what it means for an animal to be "endangered." We may get him to think about other animals that are endangered and talk about why they are endangered. If he didn't know of any, we could share some information. We might discuss what all these animals have in common. We might even talk about what it might be like if there were no more of these animals alive in the wild.

We want to nudge Nick to think big—to consider issues, not individual facts. Most likely, many of his smaller questions and related facts will fall naturally within the larger question he formulates. After giving it some thought, Nick arrived at his research question: Why are there so few pandas left in the world and what can be done to protect them?

Exploring Other Possibilities

Some of Barbara's students were not convinced that they would have a better report if it centered on one substantive question. They wanted to find answers to the list of little questions—as they had done in the past—but we were insistent that they start with a big question. Modeling, conferencing, and having students share ideas are the ways that we helped students generate worthwhile questions, but there are certainly other strategies available. Many of us have relied on the five W's (who, what, where, when, why) as a tool for formulating questions. Often, but not always, why questions and how questions lead to significant inquiry projects. This approach may be simpler and more effective for some students, especially younger ones.

Last year, Barbara used an "I Wonder" chart to get the children thinking about possible questions. After modeling this, she had students brainstorm a list of things they wondered about: When beginning a research report on Mars, for example, a student may have a list like this:

I Wonder . . .
- what it's like on Mars
- what happened to the water that used to be there
- if there was ever life on Mars
- how Earth and Mars are similar and different
- what scientists will study when they go to Mars
- why it's called the red planet

Of course, this activity will be most productive for students who have been successful in investigating appropriate resources in Stage 1: Exploring Topics. They'll have the background knowledge needed to brainstorm such a list.

Introducing Expository Text Structure

Another way to help students formulate a research question is to teach them about expository text structures. We know that research reports are structured around organizational patterns such as description, sequence, comparison and contrast, cause and effect, problem and solution, generalization and examples, question and answer, and explanation (Vacca and Vacca 1993; Devine 1987; Gunning 1998).

We focus here on five of these ways to organize expository texts: description; sequence; compare and contrast; cause and effect; and explanation. Knowledge of and appreciation for expository text structure may help students who have a broad topic but do not know how to move from this topic to a specific question. Let's suppose, for example, that a student is interested in Conestoga wagons. It may be helpful for this student to know that he could structure his question around:

- *description* (He could describe what the wagons were like and what purposes they served.)
- *sequence* (He could look at the history of the Conestoga wagon and arrange the findings chronologically.)
- *cause-and-effect pattern* (He could identify what factors caused the Conestoga wagon to lose its popularity.)
- *compare and contrast* (He could look for similarities and differences between the Conestoga wagons and another mode of transportation.)
- *explanation* (He could let the reader know that the wagons before the time of the Conestoga wagons had no brakes and then explain how the brakes on the Conestoga wagons work.)

Some students may need strategies that allow them to think about a wide range of possible perspectives through which to view their topic. Knowledge of expository text structure enables the researcher to move from a general topic to a more specific aspect of it. We'll continue to explore expository text structures in Chapter 3, where the focus will be on creating data charts around specific text structures.

☑ Checking In with Nick

Before we leave this chapter, let's touch base with Nick. You can see from his T-chart that he has already done some preliminary reading about pandas. Our conference with him led him to his research question: Why are there so few pandas left in the world and what's being done to protect them? In the next chapter, we'll follow Nick to see how he creates an organizational plan to use as he researches his big question.

CHAPTER THREE

Transforming Their Ideas into My Ideas

Getting from their ideas to my ideas is probably one of the most difficult parts of the researching and reporting process. It's the place where reading (receptive) and writing (expressive) activities unite. Up to this point, most students have been focusing primarily on reading. Now they have to cull information that pertains to their controlling idea, take notes, arrange the information in some logical sequence, synthesize ideas, claim the new understandings as their own, and report out what they've learned. This takes a great deal of planning, organization, and higher-order thinking.

In this chapter, we work through the process of (1) designing data charts, (2) taking notes, (3) recording relevant information on the charts, (4) organizing the information, and then (5) using the information to write a first draft. In other words, we'll address Stages 4 through 7 of the research and reporting process.

Stage 4: Designing a Framework for Collecting Data

Data-Retrieval Charts

There is no one right way to collect and organize data. In fact, it's probably a good idea to introduce students to several different techniques so they may eventually select the ones that are most comfortable and effective for different note-taking tasks. Students may learn how to use semantic webs and other graphic organizers, note cards, K-W-L charts (Ogle 1986), or data-retrieval charts (Clemmons and Laase 1995).

Over the years, Barbara and other teachers in her building have introduced students to many of the techniques mentioned above, but never to data-retrieval charts. After reading about them, we thought our students might benefit from the flexible structure they offer. Data-retrieval charts are organizers that help students list facts, organize them, and write summaries from their notes (Clemmons and Laase 1995). (See the template of Mary's data chart, Figure 3.1, and her completed chart, Figure 3.2.) Data charts simplify the process for recording information. Note cards can sometimes be overwhelming for upper elementary and middle school students, who put so much effort into learning how to format, code, and keep track of the cards that often the actual purpose for researching (i.e., to find answers to one's questions) takes a back seat.

Getting Ready to Organize the Data

Over the years, we've learned that the more organized the data charts are, the easier it will generally be for students to move from the data chart to a decent first draft. It is important to plan the data charts carefully and to reflect the ultimate purpose of the report in this plan. We learned this the hard way. The first time we went through the researching process, we helped students set up the data charts; everyone had the columns they needed. However, we

Figure 3.1 Mary's Data Chart Form

What beneficial and harmful things do raccoons do while interacting with humans and the environment?		
Good/Beneficial Things	**Bad/Harmful Things**	**Interesting Facts**

Used with permission from Currents in Literacy (2000).

didn't take the time to show them how to logically organize the information on the charts before they began to write; we didn't talk about the different organizational patterns expository writers use; and we didn't take the time to show them how to connect the information on the data charts. Because we neglected to do this, the students' first drafts looked just like Nick's draft (see Chapter 1); they had no underlying organizational format and they looked more like lists or jumbled collections of ideas than logically presented, well-connected ideas. We slowly realized that we needed to do more work on expository text structure before students could design their data charts. They needed to learn about different ways they could structure their reports.

We focused on five common patterns: description; sequencing; compare and contrast; cause and effect; and explanation.

- *Description*—The author paints a picture of one event, one person, one time in history, and the like. All the details in the report clarify and expand this picture.
- *Moving Through Time (Sequence)*—Each paragraph moves the reader along chronologically. Phrases such as "Five years later," "After breakfast," "At the age of ten" may be used.

Figure 3.2 Mary's Data Chart

What beneficial and harmful things do raccoons do while interacting with humans and the environment?		
Good/Beneficial Things	**Bad/Harmful Things**	**Interesting Facts**
Their meat is edible (Burt/Grossenheider)	Eat vegetables from garden (Swanson)	Related to pandas (Swanson)
Curious, fun for humans to watch (Hess)	Eat turtle eggs and bird eggs (Swanson)	Toes work like fingers: unlatches picnic baskets, unscrews jars, garbage cans (Swanson)
Are adaptable, can change when environment changes, live everywhere (Hess; MacClintock)	Steal honey from bees, think fur keeps them from getting stung (Burt/Grossenheider)	Mostly nocturnal (Burt/Grossenheider)
Eat mice (Hess)	Raid poultry yards (Burt/Grossenheider)	May dunk food in water before eating (Burt/Grossenheider)
Consume animals killed or injured by cars on highways (Hess)	Curiosity makes them bad pets (MacClintock)	Does not hibernate, lives in hollow trees, ground burrow, hollow logs (Burt/Grossenheider)

Used with permission from Currents in Literacy *(2000).*

- *Compare and Contrast*—The paragraphs are structured so that the author can identify how topics are similar and different.
- *Cause and Effect*—The author identifies a result (effect) and what led to this result (cause).
- *Explanation*—The writer clarifies why something happened or how something works.

Through these organizational patterns, authors are able to link ideas in logical ways. They can show relationships among concepts and establish the structure for the piece. When introducing the data charts to the children, we talked about the different types of organizational patterns authors use and shared books that illustrated these patterns. Then we had the students share their research questions and try to determine which text structure they would use to organize their information. We tried to schedule this discussion when support faculty (Title I, special need support services, ESL teachers, and so forth) could be in the room so that everyone received the same information. It worked well to place students into groups and have them help each other determine how to design a template for their data. Some of them came up with very clever ways to categorize information, which inspired new possibilities for others.

Setting Up Data Charts

We introduced data charts by modeling how Mary set up hers. She put her research question (*What beneficial and harmful things do raccoons do while interacting with humans and the environment?*) across the top of the page. Then she determined how she could break down the inquiry question into smaller parts. She explained that she would be using a compare-and-contrast organizing pattern. She decided that one column of her chart had to deal with the good or beneficial things raccoons do for the environment, and another column had to address the bad or harmful things. Since the students wanted to be able to include interesting information about their animals that was not related directly to their question, we added another column, "Interesting Facts." By including this column, we acknowledged that their little questions were valid and important, too. Now they had a place to record answers to the little questions they may have while researching a topic. The students' data charts clearly reflected their questions and their interests, which was wonderful to see. Let's take a look at how Chloe and Greg set up their charts.

Chloe's Data Chart

Chloe, a fifth grader, wanted to research what it is like to live in Japan so she could compare it to her life in America. She decided that she would investigate the schools, homes, and traditions. Since she also wanted a column for interesting facts, her data chart had four columns (see Figure 3.3). Interestingly, on the second page of her data chart, Chloe did not continue to include interesting facts in the fourth column. Instead, she used this column to list the reference sources she used in collecting data for the chart.

Greg's Data Chart

Greg, one of Chloe's classmates who is interested in art, was researching why Picasso had so many different styles and periods throughout his career. He broke his large question down into two smaller parts. He was going to determine what these "styles" were and how they were related to Picasso's personal life during each period. With Greg's "Interesting Facts" column, he had a total of three columns in his data chart. From the data he collected, he could draw some remarkable conclusions (see Figure 3.4).

Figure 3.3 Chloe's Data Chart

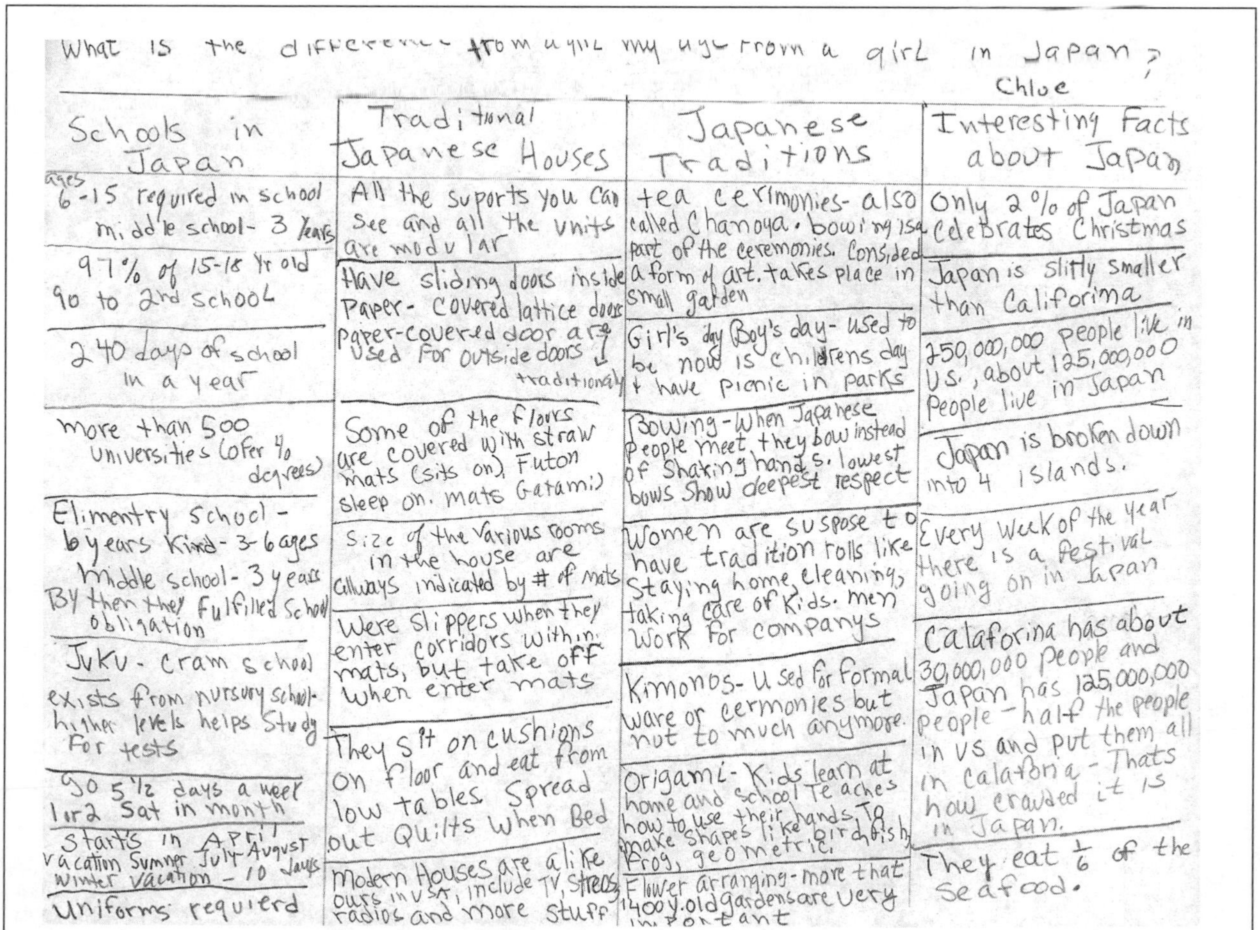

What is the difference from a girl my age from a girl in Japan?

Chloe

Schools in Japan	Traditional Japanese Houses	Japanese Traditions	Interesting Facts about Japan
ages 6-15 required in school middle school- 3 years	All the suports you can see and all the units are modular	tea cerimonies- also called Chanoya. bowing is a part of the ceremonies. Consided a form of art. takes place in small garden	Only 2% of Japan celebrates Christmas
97% of 15-18 yr old go to 2nd school	Have sliding doors inside Paper- covered lattice doors paper-covered door are used for outside doors (traditionally)	Girl's day Boy's day- used to be now is childrens day & have picnic in parks	Japan is slitly smaller than Califorina
240 days of school in a year	Some of the floors are covered with straw mats (sits on) Futon mats (sleep on. mats Gatami)	Bowing-When Japanese people meet, they bow instead of shaking hands. lowest bows show deepest respect	250,000,000 people live in US, about 125,000,000 people live in Japan
more than 500 universities (offer 4 yr degrees)	Size of the various rooms in the house are allways indicated by # of mats	Women are suspose to have tradition rolls like staying home, cleaning, taking care of kids. men work for companys	Japan is broken down into 4 islands.
Elimentry school - 6 years Kind- 3-6 ages middle school- 3 years By then they fulfilled school obligation	Were slippers when they enter corridors within mats, but take off when enter mats	Kimonos- used for formal ware or cermonies but not to much anymore.	Every week of the year there is a festival going on in Japan
Juku - cram school exists from nursury school- higher levels helps study for tests	They sit on cushions on floor and eat from low tables Spread out Quilts when Bed	Origami- Kids learn at home and school Teaches how to use their hands. To make shapes like bird, fish, frog, geometric.	Calafornia has about 30,000,000 people and Japan has 125,000,000 people - half the people in US and put them all in Calafornia - Thats how crowded it is in Japan.
go 5 1/2 days a week 1 or 2 Sat in month	Modern Houses are alike ours in USA, include TV, Streos radios and more stuff	Flower arranging- more that 1400 y. old gardens are very important	They eat 1/6 of the seafood.
Starts in April vacation Summer July-August winter vacation - 10 days			
Uniforms required			

Figure 3.4 Greg's Data Chart

	Pablo Picasso	Greg
Why did he have so many different periods?		
What were his styles of drawing?	What was his personal life like?	Interesting Facts
He had a blue period, a red period, he had cubism. *Lowery*	His red period was the time he fell in love with Fernande → 1904 Olivier 1961 married Jaqueline Roque	Changing all the time, when Picasso was 9. He made his math test into a pigeon, 1937= painted Guernica, 1961= married Jaqueline Roque, April 8 1973 = died in France, 91 years *Lowery*
Cubism, he didn't have just one style of painting *Frevert*	Had 3 children, Claude and Paloma — had Paulo *Lowery*	Spanish Artist, The "Yardstick by which other artists are judged." *Ventura*
Always changing *Lowery*	Right before the Red Period was the Blue Period He felt lonely during blue period,	Important dates— October 25, 1881 - born
Red period was when he fell in love, the blue period when he painted lonely beggars, was the lonliness he felt himself.	Fell in love with Ferande Olivier and Jaqueline Roque and Olga Koklova	1894 - showed 1st painting 1901 - began blue period 1904 - Met Olivier. Began Rose Pd 1907 - began cubism 1937 - Guernica 1947 - Claude born, 1949 - Paloma 1961 - Married Jaqueline Roque April 8, 1973 died at age 91 *Lowery*
Colors in blue period - gray, blue, white, green, etc.		

It may be helpful to see how data charts may be organized around other text structures. We've included a sample research question along with a corresponding data chart for each of the five structures we're addressing. On each data chart, you'll notice how we've separated out the big question into related smaller pieces, or subheadings. Of course, "real" data charts would probably have ten to twelve rows, rather than the two or three that we included.

1. *Description:* What kind of training do Special Olympians have to have?

Who participates	Participant qualifications	Events	Training	Interesting facts

2. *Moving Through Time (Sequence):* What were some important events in Eleanor Roosevelt's life that influenced her to become such an advocate for the underprivileged?

Early years	Adolescence	While married to FDR	After FDR's death	Interesting facts

3. *Compare and Contrast:* In what ways are Amazon parrots that live in the wild different from and similar to Amazon parrots that we keep as pets?

Wild Amazon parrots	Amazon parrot pets	Interesting facts

If students know what elements of the topic they will need to focus on to answer their question, they may be able to list them in the first column and organize the chart before they begin to collect data. For example, Mark, who researched the similarities and differences between Asian and African elephants, knew that he would be comparing and contrasting such characteristics as food, habitat, their young, enemies, and appearance. He set up his chart so that he had the list of characteristics in the first column and the similarities and differences in the next two columns. His fourth column was for interesting facts. His chart looked like this:

Characteristics	Asian elephants	African elephants	Interesting facts
Habitat			
Behavior			
Life span			

4. *Cause and Effect:* Why have school uniforms become mandatory in the Main Street Public School? In this case, the effect (result) is that students must wear uniforms. This fact can be recorded in the second column. You'd need only one box. The many causes that led to this effect could be recorded in separate boxes in the first column. (Background reading may help students identify specific subheadings for "causes." They may decide to add columns that contain data for "Academic/ School Concerns," "Parental Concerns," etc.)

Cause(s)	Effect(s)	Interesting facts

5. *Explanation:* Why does the Tasmanian devil live on a small island off the coast of Australia and no other place in the world?

Climate	Food sources	Enemies	Interesting facts

We've found that students consistently ask the same questions when creating data charts for the first time. The following list includes some of these commonly asked questions.

Frequently Asked Student Questions About Data Charts

Q: Do I need to fill up all the boxes? [or, asked in a slightly different way] Should all the columns be the same length when I'm done?

A: No. You may end up collecting different amounts of information about your various subheadings, so some columns may contain more "filled in" boxes than others. That's fine.

Q: If one column gets filled, should I carry the data over to the next column?

A: No. You should make a second data chart on a clean piece of paper that contains columns just like the ones on your original. You might want to tape the new chart to the bottom of the original so that you now have longer columns in which to store your additional data.

Q: I already know a lot about one part of my research question. Could I include a column on my chart even if I already know the answers?

A: No. The purpose of the data chart is to help you collect and organize information about your research question. The research question should be one that you don't already know the answer to and one that you are interested in finding out about.

Q: What if I don't have enough information on my data chart to begin my first draft?

A: You need to continue to gather relevant information.

Q: What if I can't find enough data to go under my headings?

A: It may be that you are struggling to find sufficient information because
  • you don't have a clear focus yet;
  • the focus is too narrow or too broad;
  • materials on the topic are too advanced; or
  • you may need to modify the question or thesis in light of the new information you are collecting. All researchers adjust their work based on what they discover as they construct new meanings. This is good; it shows that they are fine-tuning the question, making it clearer based on the new information they've found. Since knowledge is not inert, the question need not be either. Slight adjustments should be expected.

Q: When will I know if I have collected enough data?

A: When you continue to find the same answers to your question in every source you use, you probably have all the available information to answer your question.

Avoiding Pitfalls

For the most part, the children had few problems setting up their data charts, but a handful of the fifth graders had difficulty drawing their own charts. Even after modeling this on an overhead, some students found it challenging to conceptualize how to construct the boxes. For example, a few students drew lines so close together that they could not record information between them. Others knew they needed three columns, but found it difficult to divide the paper into the three fairly even columns.

To avoid confusion and frustration, you may want to prepare a few blank three-column, four-column, and five-column grids ahead of time and distribute the appropriate grids to students who need them. After using a prepared grid, students may be able to design their own the next time and customize it to their questions.

Another way to approach this may be to divide your students into small groups according to the number of columns they will be using. A knowledgeable student or another adult could lead the instruction for each small group.

Based on our experience, we suggest that students who are creating their own charts use rulers so they can make straight vertical lines. Some students feel more comfortable drawing the horizontal lines at this stage in the process. They create the whole chart before they begin to record data on it; others want to wait. They draw neat lines under each entry as they add it to the data chart. In this way, they are not limiting the amount of space they can use for each entry. You may want to demonstrate each of these approaches and explain the rationale behind each one. The important point to emphasize, however, is that the neater the chart, the easier it will be to organize the information later.

Teacher to Teacher

It may be helpful to have younger students work collaboratively on classroom data-retrieval charts before they undertake this task independently (Clemmons and Laase 1995). If, for example, you are working with third graders, you may create a blank template of a data-retrieval chart that you could tack to a wall in the room. The template may include four or five columns and four or five rows. The boxes should be just large enough to hold either three-by-five or six-by-eight-inch index cards. Answers to your questions can be recorded on these cards, which are then placed on the chart.

Since children probably won't have too much experience generating big questions, you may need to create the research question that goes at the top of the chart as well as the subcategories that appear at the top of each column. Modeling this process before you gradually release this responsibility to the children (Pearson and Gallagher 1983) provides many opportunities to show them how you formulate the questions, search for answers, record the information on the index cards, and place the cards in the correct columns. These steps may have to be repeated several times (using different research questions) until the students understand how the data charts work. Once students understand this process, you can ask them to find answers to the posed question, write their answers on the index cards, and place the cards on the appropriate space on the chart.

For beginners, the resources to use in answering this question should be available in the room. Once the chart is complete, you could model how you go from the chart to a first draft of a report. (We explain this process a bit later in this chapter.) Wouldn't it be wonderful to leave this template somewhere in the room so that students could work on researching whenever they had free time?

Stage 5: Narrowing the Search

Let's assume the students have their data-retrieval charts set up. They have written their research questions across the top of the chart, with an appropriate heading for each column. Now we're ready to enter into the next stage of researching: narrowing the search to collect specific facts and pieces of information.

According to Kuhlthau (1988), researchers in this stage use the library in different ways than they did when they were building general background knowledge about their topics. Here, the focus—or "guiding idea"—for data collection "shifts from that which is relevant to the general topic, to that which is pertinent to the focus" (p. 104). Kuhlthau (1994) reminds us that the student must start with a clear focus in order to locate information that relates to it, rather than to the broad topic from which it originated. Students return to the sources or locate additional ones. Researchers "select sources based on whether or not they are useful for answering the question, rather than on their availability or on their conforming to a predetermined opinion" (Tracey 1997, p. 5). In other words, they begin to take notes just on material that will answer their research question.

Summary Note Taking

We all know what note taking should and shouldn't look like, but teaching students how to identify and capture key ideas from texts and then reduce them to a few key words is not easy.

Over the past few years, we've tried several approaches to teach fifth graders how to take notes. The first approach we used was a very simple and effective procedure for teaching summary note taking developed by Laase (1997). The process begins by having the teacher ask the students what they already know about note taking. Our students agreed that when taking notes, they should

- record only important ideas;
- write down only key words or phrases; and
- use their own words

Next, we selected a short passage to model this note-taking process. At that time, Barbara's fifth graders were interested in mummies, so we used "Animal Mummies" (Bastian 1997), an article from an informational magazine for middle school students. Using an overhead transparency, we modeled the following steps in Laase's procedure. We cited the source and read the first paragraph to the children. Then, thinking aloud, we summarized the paragraph and underlined key words. We decided that the paragraph was mainly about What Was Mummified so we placed this heading on the chalkboard and listed the key ideas from the paragraph under it. As Laase (1997, p. 58) suggested, we followed the same steps with the next paragraph. Our heading this time was Why Mummify Animals? At this point in the lesson, we were doing all the talking. We were explaining our thinking as we went through the process. After a few paragraphs, we invited students to help, asking them to summarize the paragraphs in their own words and underline key words and phrases, which we recorded on the board. Finally, in small groups, students continued to take notes following this format.

At the end of the lesson we went back to add more ideas to our "note-taking-criteria chart."

- Identify direct quotes.
- Label the sources.
- Use codes and shorthand to eliminate the need to repeat information over and over.
- Keep notes well organized.
- Go back to the notes as soon as possible to review them and make sure they are clear.
  - Be able to read your own handwriting and shorthand. (This may not be a problem if you use portable keyboards for note taking.)
  - Indent each new note if students are not keeping note cards.

Throughout the week, Barbara referred back to this lesson. She reinforced this procedure by doing lessons from materials they were studying in various content areas. She encouraged students to use these same note-taking skills while taking notes for their data-retrieval charts.

Teacher to Teacher   Whether students are reading from reference books or downloading copies of online materials, we encourage them to use Post-its to mark a spot that contains "valuable" information. On the Post-it, they can identify in which column they will record the information.

Barbara reminded her fifth graders that since they were looking specifically for answers to their big question or for interesting facts, they could not copy chunks from resources. We've found that developmentally, some fifth graders are not yet ready to jot down single words or phrases. We've allowed some to write entire sentences to capture the author's ideas, but this is the exception rather than the rule. Of course, with additional instruction and practice, our goal is to have everyone write concise notes. Throughout this stage, we continually remind students to focus on the purpose of their research.

Support from the Librarian

This year, the librarian helped Barbara by also teaching note-taking skills. Having additional lessons on note taking reinforced the students' ability to read and choose relevant information. We modified her guidelines to be used specifically with the data charts.

Suggestions for Note Taking
1. Look at the headings of your data chart before taking notes.
2. Write only one important fact or idea in each block.
3. Make sure you use only your own words. Don't write down anything that you don't understand.
4. Come up with a way to give credit to your sources of information.
5. If your data chart is mostly filled with Interesting Facts, then you may need to refocus your research so that you find information that goes with all your headings.

Teacher to Teacher We know it isn't always possible, but it's much easier to meet the needs of all learners if you have other adults in the class when you're teaching note-taking skills. It may be worth trying to rearrange schedules to do this. Note taking is not something that most students catch on to easily. It makes a big difference to have adults who can give individual or small-group instruction while the students are working directly with their resources.

Teaching Note Taking with Technology

We began to notice that some students were printing out materials from the Internet (or other reference material) and proudly announcing, "I'm done!" They proceeded to copy the material, which was over their heads and had no meaning for them. To avoid as much of this as possible, Barbara explained from the very beginning that this "research style" was unacceptable. She talked to them about plagiarism. It is important not to squash student excitement but to channel it into productive research techniques.

Barbara often uses technology to show them how they can print out selected materials from articles and use them as resources, without taking the ideas of others and misrepresenting them as their own. There are two major parts to a typical note-taking lesson: (1) downloading material from an electronic source, and (2) demonstrating how to cull out the important information from the source.

As preparation for this lesson, Barbara selects one of the student's research topics (let's say it's the solar system) and finds an Internet site that contains information about it. Next, she sets up her classroom computer, which is linked to a large TV monitor. All the students gather around. She connects to the preselected Internet site, where she can get age-appropriate materials. She demonstrates how to choose a text that relates to the research question, copy it, and then paste it into a word processing application where it can be printed out.

For the second part of this lesson, she makes a transparency of the solar system material she downloaded. In addition, she photocopies and distributes copies of the student's data chart. Barbara reads aloud the reference material from the transparency and uses the margins of the transparency to make notations that correspond to the data chart. In the margin, she jots down key words and phrases. Since each student has his own copy of the solar system data chart, he can easily follow Barbara's explanation of how her note taking and the data chart correlate. Sometimes Barbara even color-codes the materials to correspond to the chart's subheadings. If she does this, she's careful not to highlight materials extensively, as students often have a tendency to highlight everything on the page. Students can see how they can find information that is pertinent and take notes on information that they can understand at their level.

Citing Sources

It's important for students to credit resources as they go along. You'll notice that on the data charts, we acknowledge the reference sources we used by jotting down, usually in the boxes, the last name(s) of the authors. Barbara encourages the students to devise a system to acknowledge each reference. Depending on the developmental level of your students, a simplified bibliography may be appropriate. For older students, you may want to refer them to the guidelines from the American Psychological Association (APA). The proper format for citations can be found on the APA web site: http://www.apa.org/. They have a separate URL for electronic references: http://www.apastyle.org/elecref.html. You may feel more comfortable inviting your school librarian in to teach students how to complete a bibliography. You should use whichever way works best for you and your students.

Technology Tip

There are some reputable search engines and directories (where one may search by topics) that list sites for various grade levels. KidsClick!, which was developed by librarians (http://www.sunsite.berkeley.edu/ KidsClick!/) and Yahooligans (www.Yahooligans.com), are examples of this type of engine.

If you're not familiar with these types of sites, you may be wondering how they work. Let's use Nick's research topic, pandas, to explain what he may find at one of these sites. Let's suppose Nick wants to find information about pandas that he can understand. He could open KidsClick! And go to the subtopic "Animals" under "Science and Math." Another way to get information at this site is to type the word "pandas" in the search box. In either method, he would be connected to a list of annotated sites to investigate.

When using search engines or directories, choose the option to have a summary of the sites listed, if possible. These annotations can be helpful in determining whether or not the site will provide the type of information you need to answer your question. Be careful with organizations and universities, as material may be too difficult for children to understand.

You may want to spend time with students doing whole-class lessons with the computer hooked up to a larger monitor at this point in the process as well. Through these lessons you can explain how to make a site a "favorite" or how to "bookmark" it. If students have access to the Internet, you could demonstrate how to e-mail pages to their homes so they can continue their research at home.

If you aren't as computer literate as you'd like to be, you may be able to arrange with a media specialist in your building (or even a knowledgeable student or adult) to teach a few simple lessons that will bring technology into your classroom.

Teacher to Teacher | Sites geared to children generally contain appropriate materials that are screened for a particular age. At school, Barbara's fifth graders check in with her and/or another adult before going on to new sites.

Stage 6: Recording and Organizing Relevant Data

By now, students have taken notes from their sources and have recorded the information on the data charts. The next step is to demonstrate how to organize the data before beginning the first draft.

In some cases, as students continue to read and collect data, the broader categories may be subdivided. Earlier in the chapter, we showed how Mark did this with his compare-and-contrast data chart on Asian and African elephants. Some students prefer to think about the subcategories before getting too far into the data collection. Students who have already established subcategories will probably be in pretty good shape. All they may need to do is number their information so they know what they'll write about first, second, third, and so forth. They need to think about the rationale they'll use for ordering the information as they will.

On the other hand, some students prefer to leave the categories broad and add data to the chart as they find it. These students must do more work when they begin to organize the information on the charts before writing a first draft. Mary works this way. She likes to have all the information down and then see what connections she can make among the information she's collected. Often the choice depends on the topic and the structure of the report.

You may want to make sample overheads of different types of completed data charts so students can see the range of ways in which their fellow researchers collected data. Using the charts, you can model how the information can be organized.

For students who set up their charts like Mary, with little organization built into them, the challenge will be greater. There are several ways in which this type of researcher can "code" the information. For example, Jaclyn's data chart (Figure 3.5) shows how she labeled her categories. Across the top of her

Figure 3.5 Jaclyn's Data Chart

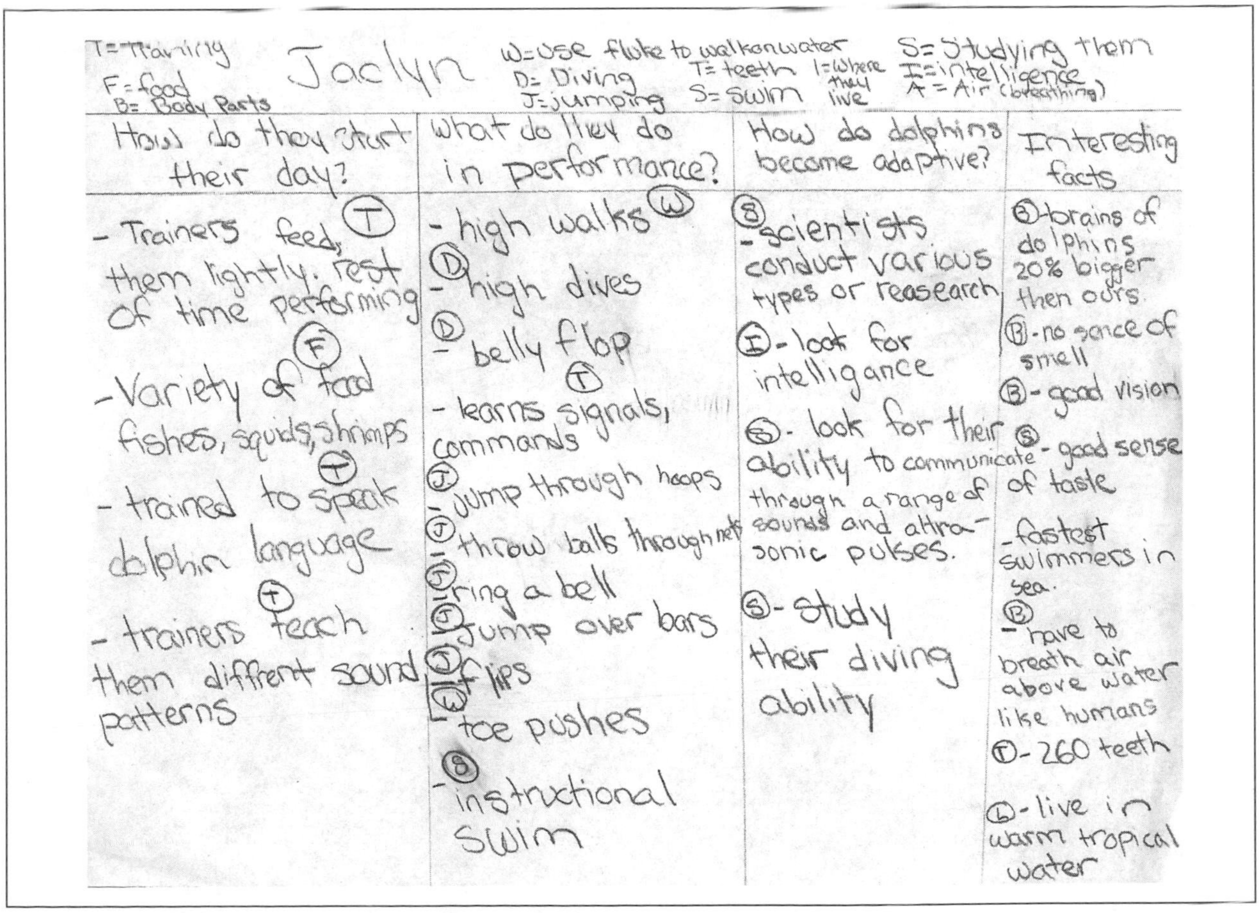
T=Training F=food B=Body Parts Jaclyn W=use fluke to walkonwater D=Diving J=jumping T=teeth S=swim I=Where they live S=Studying them I=intelligence A=Air (breathing)

How do they start their day?	What do they do in performance?	How do dolphins become adaptive?	Interesting facts
- Trainers feed, (T) them lightly. rest of time performing (F) -Variety of food fishes, squids, shrimps (T) - trained to speak dolphin language (T) - trainers teach them diffrent sound patterns	- high walks (W) (D) - high dives (D) - belly flop (T) - learns signals, commands (J) - jump through hoops (J) - throw balls through net (J) - ring a bell (J) - jump over bars (J) - flips (W) - toe pushes (S) - instructional swim	(S) - scientists conduct various types or reasearch (I) - look for intelligance (S) - look for their ability to communicate through a range of sounds and altra-sonic pulses. (S) - study their diving ability	(B) - brains of dolphins 20% bigger then ours. (B) - no sence of smell (B) - good vision (S) - good sense of taste - fastest swimmers in sea. (B) - have to breath air above water like humans (T) - 260 teeth (L) - live in warm tropical water

chart, she identifies F = food-related information; D = diving; J = jumping and so forth. In each box, she codes each item using her classification labels. Another way of doing this is illustrated in Kathryn's data chart (Figure 3.6). Kathryn first determined that the information in her second column should appear at the beginning of her report on how the universe began. She labeled her information 1A, 1B, and so forth, to indicate the order in which she would include it. Interestingly, at the bottom of her first column, after citing why others believe in the Big Bang theory, Kathryn added "My Theory" so that she would be sure to include her own hypothesis in her report.

Some students prefer to add color to indicate which items on their charts will be grouped together. Showing a variety of possible methods for organizing the data will help students find ways that feel comfortable for them.

Teacher to Teacher If students' data charts contain more information than can be recorded on one sheet of paper, remind them to record their questions on each sheet of data-chart paper to help them keep focused on the research question.

Figure 3.6 Kathryn's Data Chart

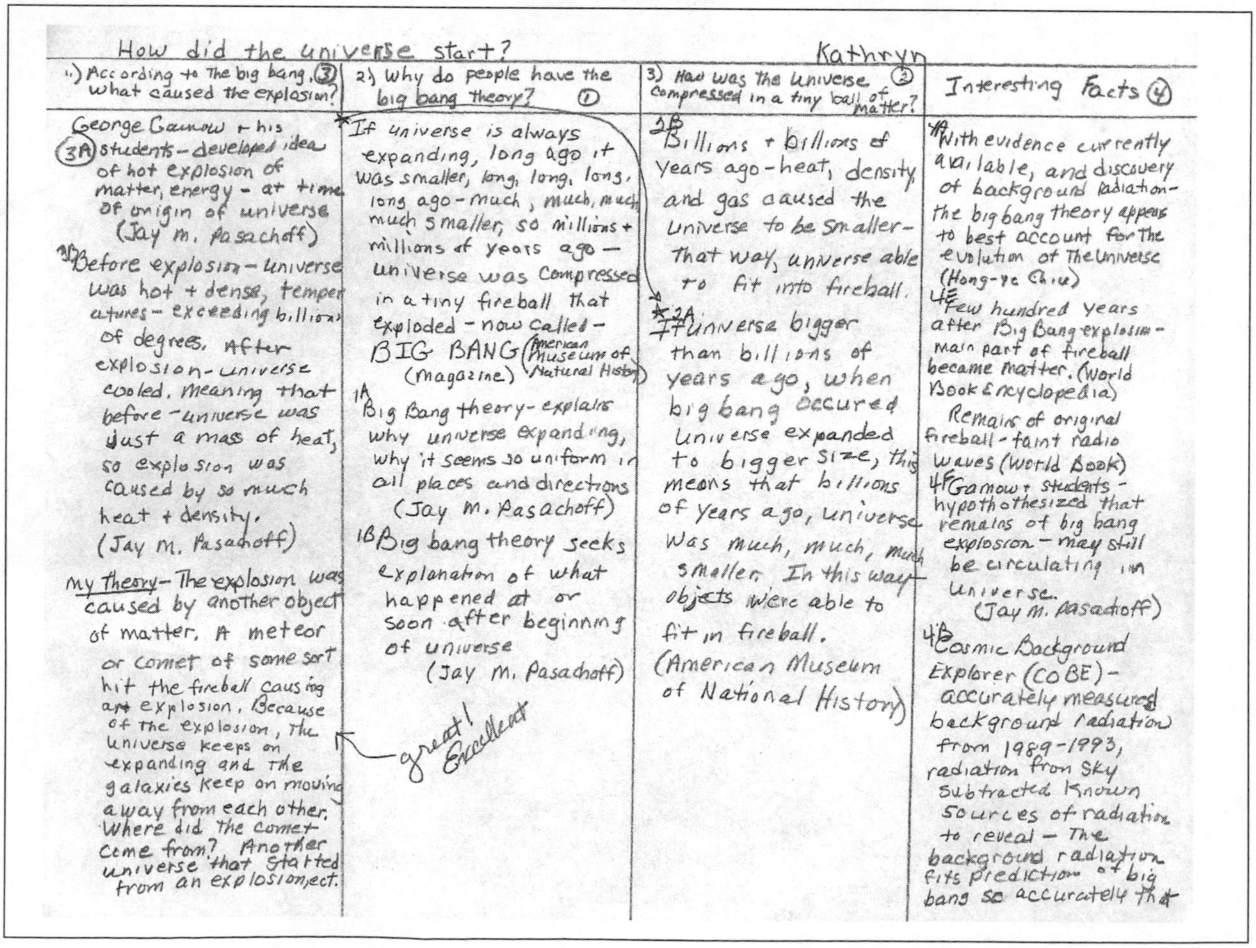

How did the universe start? Kathryn

1.) According to the big bang, (3) what caused the explosion?	2.) Why do people have the big bang theory? (1)	3) How was the universe (2) compressed in a tiny ball of matter?	Interesting Facts (4)
George Gamow + his (3A) students—developed idea of hot explosion of matter, energy—at time of origin of universe (Jay M. Pasachoff) 3B Before explosion—universe was hot + dense, temperatures—exceeding billions of degrees. After explosion—universe cooled. Meaning that before—universe was just a mass of heat, so explosion was caused by so much heat + density. (Jay M. Pasachoff) My Theory—The explosion was caused by another object of matter. A meteor or comet of some sort hit the fireball causing an explosion. Because of the explosion, the universe keeps on expanding and the galaxies keep on moving away from each other. Where did the comet come from? Another universe that started from an explosion, ect.	*If universe is always expanding, long ago it was smaller, long, long, long, long ago—much, much, much much smaller, so millions + millions of years ago—universe was compressed in a tiny fireball that exploded—now called—BIG BANG (American Museum of Natural History) (Magazine) 1A Big Bang theory—explains why universe expanding, why it seems so uniform in all places and directions (Jay M. Pasachoff) 1B Big bang theory seeks explanation of what happened at or soon after beginning of universe (Jay M. Pasachoff) great! Excellent	2B Billions + billions of years ago—heat, density and gas caused the universe to be smaller—That way, universe able to fit into fireball. *2A If universe bigger than billions of years ago, when big bang occured universe expanded to bigger size, this means that billions of years ago, universe was much, much, much smaller. In this way objects were able to fit in fireball. (American Museum of National History)	4A With evidence currently available, and discovery of background radiation—the big bang theory appears to best account for the evolution of the universe (Hong-ye Chiu) 4E Few hundred years after Big Bang explosion—main part of fireball became matter. (World Book Encyclopedia) Remains of original fireball—faint radio waves (World Book) 4F Gamow + students—hypothothesized that remains of big bang explosion—may still be circulating in universe. (Jay M. Pasachoff) 4B Cosmic Background Explorer (COBE)—accurately measured background radiation from 1989–1993, radiation from sky subtracted known sources of radiation to reveal—The background radiation fits prediction of big bang so accurately that

Stage 7: Going from Data to First Draft

Going through the process of transforming data into a written draft with fifth graders taught us that it's essential to take time to model each step before asking students to try something on their own. It may seem as if upper elementary and middle school students should be able to make this transition from data chart to first draft without much help, but taking time to model how you would make this shift is important.

Before Barbara begins this stage with her students, she sends another letter home to parents to keep them informed (see Figure 3.7). In it, she lets

Figure 3.7 Barbara's Letter Informing Parents of the Writing Process

---

November 5, 2001

Dear Parents,

We are about to begin Phase 2 of the research inquiry project. By tomorrow, your children will have completed the note-taking phase. I plan on showing them how they can move from their data chart, where they have collected their notes, to writing a first draft. I will ask students to finish their first draft by Tuesday, November 13.

After this initial first draft, I will work on teaching various strategies that the students can use in their reports. In that way, I can guide them on how to make revisions so that their reports are well organized and their thoughts flow smoothly from one sentence to another. I will help them to incorporate leads so as to make their writing more exciting. This second draft will not be due until Friday, December 7. Although that seems like a long time, Thanksgiving recess and school dismissals at 11:15 A.M. [for parent conferences] do limit available teaching time. Their final reports with all revisions and corrections in regard to spelling and grammar will be due on Friday, December 14. I will explain to the students later exactly what the final report is to contain.

I also want students to prepare visual presentations to go along with their reports. They may be models, dioramas, three-dimensional representations, or any other appropriate examples that illustrate one aspect of the research paper. I do not want students to begin this undertaking until the second draft is completed on December 7 although they should be thinking about ideas for this earlier. Presentations will be made on Tuesday, December 18, through Thursday, December 20.

I really appreciate all your support. Please continue to have your children work nightly on their writing. Some students may find that they may need to go back and do more research if they have not collected enough notes. This process will be a good learning experience that they will continue to use throughout their school years.

In summary, the dates are:

First draft due: Tuesday, November 13

Second draft due: Friday, December 7

Final report due: Friday, December 14

Visual presentations: Tuesday, December 18 through Thursday, December 20.

(Do not start visual presentations until December 7 but be thinking about them earlier.)

Like last time, I will enclose calendars to help with the planning. Please keep one set at home. Do not hesitate to contact me at any time if you have any questions or concerns.

Sincerely,

Barbara S. Siegel

- -

I have seen the letter of Monday, November 5, concerning Phase 2 of the research project.

_____

Parent Signature

Questions:

---

them know the time line and explains that the students will be preparing a visual to accompany their research paper.

Heading in the Right Direction

Once students organize the data charts in some logical fashion, it's time to focus more directly on the writing component of researching and reporting.

They know that the introduction will consist of an engaging lead, perhaps some information from the "Interesting Facts" column on the data chart, and the research question. Mary used a think-aloud to model how she got started on her raccoon report, but she reminded students that getting started is the important point. They should know what they need to include in the lead, but they also need to realize that the lead at this time is tentative at best. We'll come back to work on it—to polish it up—later.

Since the students are now aware of several lead strategies—through read-alouds of picture books and through direct instruction—they may already have some ideas for the type of lead they'd like to write (see Chapter 5). Using an overhead of her data chart, Mary shared her thinking and a lesson that went something like this:

> Before I begin to write, I'll need to reread my research question [which she does]. I know I'll be comparing and contrasting what the raccoon does that humans like and don't like. I'll have to note this in my lead. I've been thinking that I might try the "Hanging On" strategy. Remember how the author of *Do They Scare You?* [Collard 1992] used it when he described "Giant Squids"? I liked that and think it might work well for me here. I'll include some interesting facts, too, to pique my reader's curiosity.

Mary would continue by drafting a lead and putting it on the overhead. It's far from perfect. That's exactly what she wants to model. She continues with her lesson by explaining that

> I don't want to get bogged down in the lead. This first draft isn't my final draft. I'll need to come back to it and make revisions, based on where the rest of the report takes me.

Once Mary has a lead paragraph drafted, she turns her attention to her data chart (see Figure 3.2). She has two columns in her chart (not including the "Interesting Facts"). She rereads aloud her research question and looks over her chart. She decides to begin her report with the second column and explains her rationale for doing so. Next, she models how she would convert the heading of the second column into a lead sentence. She also needs to use this lead sentence to transition from the first paragraph into this one. She uses the "Although" strategy: "Although these masked animals are cute [an idea that was mentioned in the first paragraph], they can be harmful to humans and the environment."

Before beginning to write about the ways in which raccoons harm the environment, Mary takes the time to organize the information in the column and explains why she's arranging the data this way. She wants the students to know that there should be a logical progression of ideas. Once the data are logically ordered, she's ready to begin this paragraph. As she writes, she demonstrates how to elaborate on each fact, so the report doesn't sound like a list of isolated ideas. Finally she models how she would check each item off the chart as she uses it.

The important part of this demonstration is to model what we want to emphasize. That is, students need to be thinking about the organization of the report before they begin to write. They need to be aware of the structure of the report and the links they are going to use to move logically from one idea to the next. We develop this idea more fully in the next chapter, when we address transitions and organizational structures.

Possible Pitfalls

Transitioning from the data chart to the first draft is not always easy for students. Before beginning this process, you may want to consider some of the pitfalls we've encountered along the way.

Pitfall No. 1

When beginning to compose their first draft, many students ignore their data chart. Some think their data have been collected so now they can write from memory. Others don't realize that they are supposed to keep referring back to the data chart; perhaps they think this is cheating.

Solution: Remind students that they should be constantly referring to the chart and checking off data they have used in the report.

Pitfall No. 2

Students think they need to take each piece of information off the chart in the order in which it was recorded, beginning with information found in the top left box and concluding with the lower right box.

Solution: Explain that the purpose of the data chart is to record information; it's up to the writer to determine in which order the information should be shared with the reader. Model different ways to arrange the data, not necessarily beginning with data from the first column.

Pitfall No. 3

Students may create a well-organized paragraph using the information from one column and then get stuck. They may not be able to begin the next paragraph, or the paragraphs may not seem related.

Solution: They need to be introduced to transition strategies so they can create "bridges" for their ideas (see Chapter 4).

Pitfall No. 4

As soon as it's time to begin to move from the data chart to the first draft, scores of students need to use the bathroom, sharpen pencils, go back to resources for more information, or act out in more aggressive ways.

Solution: A colleague of ours, Sue Fleming, is constantly on the lookout for these types of behavior. They often signal avoidance strategies. (As adults in similar situations, we often decide it's time to clean the house, do some baking, or run errands.) Acknowledge that the process is difficult for students and explain why they are using these avoidance tactics. For students having an especially difficult time getting started, have them dictate to you while you write. You can cue them with questions about their topic and model some of the lead strategies for them.

Pitfall No. 5

Students using the explanation text structure provide the explanation in the first paragraph. The report is done in one paragraph. This type of experience may occur with other forms of writing as well.

Solution: Instead of telling all in the opening paragraph, show students how to present one idea, provide details, elaborate, and then transition into the next paragraph (i.e., the next idea).

☑ Checking In with Nick

The last time we visited with Nick, he was in the process of forming his research question, which became, Why are there so few pandas left in the world and what can be done to protect them? At this point, he knows a great deal about expository text structure. He's decided that in order to answer this question, he'll use an explanation organizational structure.

After thinking back on what he already knew about pandas from his preliminary readings, he chose to include three subheadings on his data chart (see Figure 3.8): Why were pandas killed?; What's being done?; and Interesting facts. He collected information and took notes that related directly to his research question. He's already given some thought to his lead and thinks he will hook the reader by including the facts about the panda's weight at birth and how much food they can consume daily. Although he wants to start with these facts, he's not sure which strategy he'll use. He's thinking about trying the "Imagine" strategy. He knows he has to talk about his research question in the lead paragraph, too, so his readers will know where he's headed.

Figure 3.8 Nick's Data Chart

Why were pandas killed?	What's being done?	Interesting facts	References
Can be killed by leopards or wild dogs	Grow more bamboo (2)	Weighs 2 oz. at birth	Eberle, I. 1973. *Pandas Live Here.*
Used to live in mts. and valleys but built houses and farms (3)	Chinese govt. protect land (1)	Makes 6'4" 190–275 lbs.	Fowler, A. 1995. *Giant Pandas: Gifts from China.*
Kill for fur (1)	Send some to zoos to protect—mostly in China (3)	Rare—only in southwestern China	Gross, R. B. 1972. *A Book About Pandas.* Hoffman, A. 1983. *Animals in the Wild: Panda.*
Some die on way to zoo (4)	In zoos—carefully planned diets: give vitamins; cool and dark like original homes; water to cool off (4)	Adults eat 30 lb. bamboo daily	Horton, C. 1996. *Endangered Bears.*
Scientists want to study them when first discovered (2)		Spends 12 hours/day eating	
		Bear or raccoon?	
		Good climbers but like to stay on ground	
		1,000 in wild; 100 in zoos	

It makes most sense for Nick to begin with the information in the first column of his data chart, but not all of Nick's classmates will want to do this. Nick decided to number the data in each column in the order in which he expects to use them in his first draft.

You'll notice that not all the boxes are filled in. That's fine. Some of the columns contain more information than others. That's to be expected. You'll notice that when Nick writes his report, he will not use all the data he collected. That's fine, too. He has to determine what gets included in the final report and what he'll leave out. Nick also kept track of the resources he used. He recorded them in the fourth column of his data chart. Since Nick believes he has enough information to answer his question and his data are logically organized, he's ready to begin his first draft.

What's Next?

Nick has already completed the first seven stages of researching and reporting:

Stage 1: Exploring Topics
Stage 2: Knowing What You Know (and Don't Know)
Stage 3: Formulating a Research Question
Stage 4: Designing a Framework for Collecting Data
Stage 5: Narrowing the Search
Stage 6: Recording and Organizing Relevant Data
Stage 7: Going from Data to First Draft

Part 2 of this book represents Stage 8 of this process (Revising Drafts). We'll look at Stage 9, Presentation, which is the final stage, at the end of Chapter 6.

Going through this progression of activities alongside the fifth graders led us into areas of teaching and learning that we never would have thought about otherwise. Our own modeling slowed down the process for us—we had to continually evaluate what was working for us and for the students and what wasn't. Having our own questions and our own data charts with what we wanted to find out sustained us. The ideas of the others who were sharing this process pushed us on. In Part 2 of the book, we share some of the strategies we developed to help students improve the quality of their nonfiction writing.

PART TWO

Revising and Assessing

Our first attempt at moving the children from the data charts to a first draft led to reports that lacked voice and passion. They didn't quite sound like encyclopedias, but they definitely weren't page-turners. The leads were basically all the same: "I'm writing a report about [topic]." The transitions, if used, were often ineffective. Disconnected thoughts jumped out at the reader. Typically, the reports ended with "I hope you liked reading my report."

We knew the students were capable of writing much better reports. We also knew that giving the same advice as we always did (e.g., "The lead has to hook the reader" or "You need to include more transitions to connect all the good ideas you have") was not working. We asked ourselves what else we should be doing to make this advice more meaningful. By researching and writing our own reports, we understood the feeling of helplessness that students face when they realize that their writing is not well done but don't know how to make it better. It slowly dawned on us that telling students what the end product should be like (e.g., have an interesting lead, conclude with a strong closing statement), was not enough; we needed to *show* them *how* to craft their writing to get to these desired final products. Our job was to create more relevant instructional lessons!

Necessity Is the Mother of Invention

We began to search for examples of strategies other writers use for leads, but the resources we found were limited. Out of desperation, we began to analyze what published nonfiction authors did and then taught the students to use these same strategies in their writing. For example, we noticed that many authors begin expository writing by posing a thought-provoking question.

We shared examples we found in children's magazines and modeled a few of our own. We talked about "good" (open-ended) and "boring" (one-word answer) questions. The fifth graders were already familiar with this from lessons we did with them to formulate their research questions. We asked the children to try out this strategy with their topics. This process differed from what we'd done in the past in one small but very significant way. Instead of just sharing samples to show what good leads sounded like, we tried to break down the process and to decipher what the author had done to create it. We attempted to explain why the leads were effective and, *specifically,* what made them work. Our initial results were amazing. We were off and running!

Introducing questions as a strategy for writing leads was fairly straightforward. Let's consider what you might do to introduce a strategy that is not as obvious. Let's pretend, for example, that we want students to be able to replicate the strategy used in the following lead: "Like the Energizer Bunny, the contest between Vice President Al Gore and Texas governor George W. Bush just keeps on going and going" ("A Surprise Ruling in Florida," *Time for Kids,* 15 December 2000). In the past, we may have read this sentence to the students and briefly talked about what made this an interesting hook. We may have said something like, "Isn't this a great lead? It really hooks the reader. Wasn't it clever of the author to compare the dragged-out election to this famous bunny?"

Unfortunately, these presentations were often too abstract or too fleeting to produce lasting results. Sometimes we would "walk through" a series of similarly effective leads in one lesson. Even if students did agree that they were terrific leads, not many of them could determine what the authors had done and apply the processes to their own writing. We slowly came to realize that in order for students to use the strategies effectively, they would need to begin by fastening their understandings to something tangible. As a result, we not only introduced the leads and held discussions, we also dissected the leads and tried to determine what the authors had done to make them memorable. Then we went one step further and named each strategy.

With the Energizer Bunny example, we might have begun the lesson the same way we did in the past by saying, "Isn't this a great lead? It really hooks the reader. Wasn't it clever of the author to compare the dragged-out election to this famous bunny?" but we wouldn't have stopped there. We would have introduced the term "simile" if the students weren't familiar with it. We would have explained how the author of the "bunny lead" had used a simile and then would have presented other examples of comparisons made with the word "like" or "as." We could have started by creating similes for common objects and then gradually demonstrated how the students could use this strategy with their research topics. If, for instance, a student were researching the invention of the automobile, we could suggest the following lead: "The early automobiles crawled along the unpaved streets like ants on their way to a picnic." If someone were writing about the big bang theory, a lead with a simile might be, "I wonder if the earth's beginning was like a giant Fourth of July fireworks display?" After further discussion, we might propose that we call this strategy "Dare to Compare." We may conclude by having them try to create a simile for their own research topics. The goal for these strategy lessons is to demystify the processes used by published authors and to translate these processes into language that upper elementary and middle school students can understand and apply.

The students were excited. They seemed to actually like playing with different options. Now they had specific ways to help them shape their ideas. Writing was still hard work for the majority of students, but the fresh, new challenges we set before them seemed to reenergize them. And energy is definitely what's needed when one thinks about revision.

We continued to use this process of finding and analyzing strategies authors use for transitions, lead, and conclusions. We attached a label to each one so that all of us could use a common language when discussing them.

Instructional Methods

We usually selected four or five strategies to introduce during each lesson, but this may vary depending on the students with whom you work and the type of expository writing in which they are engaged. You may need to teach each strategy separately, or you may be able to introduce several at one time. We began each lesson with these four steps:

1. Announce the strategy's title and ask the students to brainstorm what they think this strategy will be like.
2. Give a description of the strategy, confirming what the students hypothesize from step one, if they were correct.
3. Share an example from a children's expository magazine on an overhead, giving each student a handout that contains a copy of the example.
4. Present examples of students' work that demonstrates how they have applied the strategy in their writing.

Matching Writers and Strategies

It is important to give students the support they need to be successful. To ensure that all students met with success, we intentionally matched each person with two or three specific strategies that were appropriate for her particular project.

Our decisions regarding which students should try which strategies were based on each student's topic, how the student was organizing the information (text structure), his development as a writer, and his ability to use language to express complex ideas.

Barbara made a set of handouts. Each page contained the name of a strategy and an example of how it was used by a children's magazine author. In addition, Barbara listed across the bottom of each page the names of students for whom the strategy might be appropriate. She also included specific notes to students. Barbara color-coded the handouts so her students would be able to locate them easily in their writing folders. Yellow paper, for example, was used to photocopy lead strategies, while green was used for transitions and pink for conclusions.

Often we would group children who might benefit by being introduced to a specific strategy. For example, we might meet with a group of students who are strong creative writers and say,

> I know you have great imaginations. I wonder if you could hook your readers into your reports by using the "Imagine," the "Hanging On," or the "Question" strategy. Let me explain how each of these works and give you some examples to think about. Perhaps you could try out one of them—or maybe all of them—and see which works best.

Students responded favorably and enjoyed the challenge of exploring different types of strategies.

During many lessons, we asked students to share their leads while other members of the class named the strategy that they chose. These developing writers were eager to do so. Sometimes they presented in small groups; at other times they came together as a large group. Listening to one another and providing immediate feedback was extremely important. It served as positive reinforcement to motivate others to take risks and try out new strategies. Frequently, we asked the child to read a few sentences from the first draft and the revision, noting the effect created by the changes made and how improved the writing was as a result. Students need to know their efforts pay off. These sharing sessions also illustrated the many possible ways to write effectively and enabled us to review strategies in an engaging, authentic setting.

Part 2 examines specific strategies that authors may use to write or revise expository texts. We've grouped them into strategies for transitions, leads, and conclusions. These strategies are also listed in Appendix D, for the reader's convenience. We hope you'll pick and choose the ones you think may help your students grow as writers of expository texts.

What's the Connection?
Transitions and
Organizational Structures

Purposeful transitions guide readers to key points and conclusions.
—Spandel and Stiggins, *Creating Writers*

During our student teaching days, we were often reminded by our supervisors to focus on transitions. They wanted us to make sure students moved from activity to activity without wasting time or causing too much havoc. It wasn't enough to have an outstanding activity; we needed to transition students into and out of the activity "seamlessly." Today, many years since our supervised student teaching, we still hear teachers saying things like, "If you're wearing blue today, please walk to the rug." Or "If your writing folder is yellow, you may place it back in the milk crate now." These simple statements help teachers move students around the room in a systematic, orderly fashion. When we write, we have a similar job: to move the reader along from idea to idea in a logical progression.

It may seem strange to talk about transitions before talking about leads. As writers, we usually think about how important it is to get those first words down, to hook the reader with a compelling lead. We agree that the leads are important, and we do give students strategies to get started, but we don't emphasize them at this point. We haven't formally introduced lead strategies yet. That comes a bit later. Since we've been informally introducing them through our read-alouds of nonfiction books and through class discussions, some students will have strong leads already. But students who are not satisfied with their leads shouldn't worry about them now. They've had enough exposure to leads so they shouldn't feel as if they are facing a blank page without any resources. We'll come back to work on leads again once we organize our ideas.

As students begin their first drafts, we'd rather they focus their attention on the overall organization of their reports and on the transitions within the report that help create coherence. We've found that emphasizing these elements early in the process helps students stay focused on their topic. It also cuts down on the amount of revisions they need to make later on in the process. Once the relationship among ideas is evident, writers can transition logically from one idea to another with less effort than it takes to do so when the structure is lacking. We found this out the hard way in a writing task Barbara assigned her students. In an e-mail to Mary, she reflected on the results: "Teaching transitions will be a lot easier if the organizing principle is established firmly. I found this out after I read all the first drafts tonight."

Many of the papers Barbara was reading looked like the first draft of Nick's panda report; they were simply a list of facts. Our friend Jeri Gillin calls this type of writer "The Lister" (Gillin 2002). When "The Lister" writes, ideas are developed only slightly, if at all. There are no connections, merely one fact after another.

Other papers contained more detailed information, but the information was scattered randomly throughout the paper. Jeri calls this type of writer "The Repeater" (Gillin 2002). These writers repeat facts in three or four places. They don't reread what they have written, and whenever an idea comes into their heads, it appears in the paper. Sometimes "The Repeater" repeats facts because they are important and she wants her reader to know this; other times it's to use up space and make the report longer. Most times, however, the writer isn't even aware she's doing this.

It's not uncommon for students to have trouble with organization and transitions. Silverman, Hughes, and Wienbroer (1999) note that they may simply need to "juggle the order [of the points they want to make] so that one point leads logically to the next" (p. 78). This step should come before students start to draft the paper. They can "juggle" the ideas by rearranging their note cards or using a system to code the items on the data chart (see Chapter 3).

Teacher to Teacher We can probably all name students whose papers lack a logical progression of ideas. Barbara has "The Listers" and "The Repeaters" reread each paragraph, one at a time. After reading each paragraph, they identify the topic(s) in it. Next, they list the topics in the margin beside the paragraph. From this activity, they can see if they have several topics in one paragraph or if they have repeated the same piece of information in more than one place. During a recent conference, Barbara went through this process with one of her fifth graders. This girl was writing about a day she spent with her grandmother. The paragraph started with how her grandmother watched while the granddaughter went swimming and was freezing from the water. The next sentence jumped to the grandmother and student eating cold ice cream. We've all read stories like this. We can appreciate what the child was thinking when it was written, but we're always filling in gaps. During the writer's conference, Barbara helped the girl notice how she had changed subjects. With a little thought, she was able to connect the two ideas by stating that "despite being cold, she and her grandmother ate delicious chocolate ice cream."

Simon (1988) recommends that students write outlines to help them organize their ideas. He notes that drafting an outline before writing a paper does not ensure that the paper will be logical. If, however, the author writes an outline after the piece is finished, he should be able to tell what the main point of each paragraph is and how each relates to the entire paper.

Connecting Ideas

When using data charts, the challenge becomes making "bridges" (Silverman, Hughes, and Wienbroer 1999) *within* a column and *between* two of the columns on the chart. Writers can create these bridges in several ways. Sometimes it's as simple as adding a word to signal the reader. Ploeger (2000) notes that specific words may help the reader know what the writer is about to do. For instance, he may be getting ready to

- signal a sequence in time, between events, or from one step to the next in a procedure (e.g., first, next, later)
- make comparisons (e.g., similarly, likewise, also)
- show contrasts (e.g., on the other hand, conversely)
- extend ideas or add examples (e.g., in addition, moreover)
- indicate a dramatic shift in thinking (e.g., however, but, yet)
- conclude or summarize (e.g., in sum, finally, lastly)

Many of us have probably given students lists of transition words, but we may have neglected to teach them about the underlying relationship these words signal. That's the important part. The young writers need to know what function these words serve before they can use them effectively.

Delving Deeper

Peters (1985) notes, "Signals are particularly important at the beginning of a paragraph, where readers are predisposed to receive a change or new development of the topic" (p. 98). Peters continues by suggesting that these signals may indicate that the discussion is "about to become broader or more specific" (p. 98). Often, traditional transition words work well to link ideas, but sometimes we need to do more than add a word to make connections.

One morning, Mary was working with Barbara's fifth graders. She had her raccoon data chart (see Figure 3.2) on an overhead and was using the analogy of "bridges" to explain transitions (Silverman, Hughes, and Wienbroer 1999). She had just begun when Kevin, an astute fifth grader, raised his hand. He noticed that Mary had the word "curious" in both columns on her chart ("good/beneficial things raccoons do" and "bad/harmful things raccoons do"). He wondered if we could somehow use the word "curious" to bridge her "bad/harmful" column into her "good/beneficial" column. He suggested that we use the word "curious" in the last sentence of one paragraph and then repeat it in the first sentence of the next paragraph. Kevin was a step ahead of us. He had already figured out an effective strategy to use. We called this one Repeat a Word. You'll find it and several others listed later in this chapter.

Avoiding Possible Pitfalls

Once students are familiar with transition strategies, they may overuse the same one(s). For example, Earl found it easy to end each paragraph with a question. The first three paragraphs of his book report on Egypt ended with questions: "How do we know all that information about ancient times?" "Do you know who owned all the land?" "Did the pharaoh own everything?" Overreliance on one strategy is not necessarily bad. It does show that the student is thinking about making connections for his reader. That's important. While using one effective strategy is a good place to start, we can't stop there. We need to make sure that Earl and students like Earl learn other strategies that work for them, too.

When Barbara observes a child overusing one strategy, she has him reread the paper and count up how many times he used the same strategy. She might even have him jot down, in the margin, the names of all the strategies he used and then count them. The student usually realizes that one strategy predominates. Barbara can then review other possible strategies.

It's important for students to know that they don't need to start each paragraph with a transition word or strategy. And they shouldn't. An overdependence on transitional devices can interfere with the flow of ideas. The writing gets bogged down and stilted. In many cases, the logical progression of ideas is all that's needed to meld a piece together. You'll be able to convey this idea best by reading texts aloud and discussing ways in which authors move the reader from idea to idea.

Teacher to Teacher   Barbara color-codes the strategies so students can find them easily in their writing folders. For instance, you may want to code all the transition handouts blue, lead handouts yellow, and so forth. We've also found that, whenever possible, it's best to teach and practice the strategies when other professionals are in the room so they can provide individual or small-group instruction.

Strategies to Connect One Paragraph to the Next

1. Repeat a Word

The author uses a word in the last sentence of a paragraph and then again in the first sentence of the next paragraph to link the paragraphs.

Example: Notice how Andrews, the author of this article about a military vehicle, repeats the word "power" to make this smooth transition:

> The [Light Armored Vehicle-25] is more than five and a half feet longer, two feet taller, a foot wider, and more than 17,000 pounds heavier than a Humvee. The new vehicle was built to get people to battle quicker and give them more power.
> And power this vehicle has: a 25-millimeter chain gun, one machine gun and another free-hand machine gun on top for the commander . . .
> T. Andrews, "Rough Rider," *Boys' Life*, March 2000, 17.

Student Examples: This is a fairly easy strategy for all students to use. Can you find which word Chad, a fourth grader, repeats as he moves from one paragraph to another in his report on Mercury? He concludes one paragraph with

> There is no liquid water on Mercury, but scientists think that there is ice in Mercury's craters. There also is little gravity.
> Mercury has a weak magnetic field and it also has weak gravity. Mercury has little atmosphere because of its weak gravity. [Chad continues to provide information about Mercury's atmosphere in this paragraph.]

Kathryn adds to the complexity of this basic strategy by combining it with another strategy, "Begin a Paragraph with a Question," (see Strategy No. 4) in her report that explains how the earth began. This fifth grader writes:

> After being packed into the fireball for so long, the main part of our Big Bang theory occurred. The explosion!

What explosion? Thousands and thousands of years ago, a man named George Gamow and his students developed an idea of a hot explosion of matter and energy . . .

Teacher to Teacher This is a relatively easy strategy for students to master. Relying too heavily on it, however, can make the writing seem stilted. Some students may not realize they are overusing it. Try having them circle the repeating words between paragraphs with a colored pen to help them become aware of how frequently they use this strategy.

2. Use Related Words

This is similar to Repeat a Word, but instead of repeating the exact word, an author may use a related word, often a synonym.

Example: Notice how this author uses the words "to honor" at the end of one paragraph and continues this idea by choosing "paid tribute to" in the first sentence of the next paragraph in this article about the veterans of Pearl Harbor.

> Some of this year's heroes—New York City rescue workers—gathered in Hawaii to honor the heroes of decades before.
> President Bush paid tribute to the veterans.
> "Remembering Pearl Harbor," *Time for Kids,* 14 December 2001, 2.

Student Example: Sometimes varying the word choice adds freshness to the writing. For example, Nora uses the term "water pollution" at the end of one paragraph and begins a new paragraph with "Water contamination . . ."

Teacher to Teacher If the class is working on similar topics, brainstorm some synonyms for terms commonly used. For example, in writing an autobiography, students might interchange "holiday" for "vacation" and "interests" for "hobbies."

3. End a Paragraph with a Question

The author ends the paragraph with an interesting question and then begins to address this question in a new paragraph.

Example: The author of this article about Mars poses a question to make a smooth transition from her second to third paragraph.

Take the idea of extraterrestrial life—things that don't live on Earth. If you've seen any old Martian movies, you know that Mars has long been a favorite place to locate all types of extraterrestrials. How come?

"We're interested in Mars because we're next to it," says Pascal Lee, planetary scientist at NASA Ames Research Center. Plus, Mars is covered with soil and rocks like Earth. "When we look at the landscape of Mars, it looks familiar. This feeds our imaginations," Lee adds.

N. Finton, "Visions of Mars," *National Geographic for Kids!*, March 2002, 18–22.

Student Example: Armand poses a question that makes us uneasy, but we love his answer. He leads into his concluding paragraph by writing: "But why am I even taking time to write this autobiography?" His last paragraph reads: "Well, the answer is that I want to have something to remember when I'm older and can't remember my childhood. I can then take this autobiography and look at the pages. I would remember all those good times with relish, wanting to be a kid again. Does that answer the question?"

Teacher to Teacher Good questions can be used for leads, transitions, or conclusions. They keep the reader actively engaged in the text. Be careful, nevertheless, that the student doesn't overdo this strategy.

4. Begin a Paragraph with a Question

The author begins with a question that moves the reader to a new point.

Example: The author of this article about Hurricane Floyd concludes the introductory paragraph with a statement, then begins the next paragraph with a question.

Nearly 3 million people along the East Coast had been ordered to pack up and get out last week. It was the biggest evacuation in U.S. history.

What evil force could possibly drive so many people from their homes? [In this paragraph, the author continues to describe Hurricane Floyd and the damage it caused.]

"A Monster Hurricane," *Time for Kids*, 24 September 1999, 4–5.

Student Example: Catherine makes it easy for her reader to follow her line of thinking while using this strategy in her report about white-tailed deer. In one paragraph, she notes where deer can be found and the type of environment that most deer find appealing. She concluded this paragraph with: "They don't usually live in the Western part of the continent because some of the deer's worst enemies live there." She begins the next paragraph with this question:

"What are other factors that affect the deer population?" In this paragraph she describes how the winter weather impacts the lives of deer.

The students need to understand that new information is coming and that "old" facts are not going to be rehashed.

5. Contrast

A new paragraph begins by stating how the main idea of this paragraph is related to, but dissimilar from, the main idea of the last paragraph. Words such as "conversely," "in contrast," or "on the other hand" may be used to signal this shift.

Example: Members of the U.S. Olympic Committee have high hopes for several U.S. gold medals in the 2002 Winter Olympics. Several paragraphs in this article highlight the chances of this happening. Partway through the article, however, there is a shift away from the emphasis on high achievement to a need for the athletes to have fun and to enjoy making new friends. The shift takes place in this paragraph:

> Despite the fierce competition of the Games, Olympic organizers want participants to relax and get to know their fellow athletes. [Notice how the word "despite" is used to signal the contrast.]
>
> R. Upadhyay, "Off to the Olympics," *Time for Kids,* 1 February 2002, 4–6.

Student Example: Each time we have students research a topic, we're amazed at how many of them organize their reports around the compare-and-contrast text structure. Erin tackles this text pattern by contrasting two types of dragons. She first describes the fire-breathing dragon and then transitions into the next paragraph by writing "Practically the opposite of the species of Fire Breathing dragon is the unique long line of Water dragons."

It's important for students to know what type of transition words signal a contrast: "but," "although," "even though," "still," "however," "while," "yet."

6. "Although"

Writers begin a paragraph with "Although" to let the reader know a different idea is being introduced.

Example: See how the author of this article about children from the Mohawk Nation applies this strategy to transition from several paragraphs in which she talks about the pride the children of the Mohawk Nation take in their Native language and in their Native names, in particular.

> Although their pride in their heritage is strong, these students can't neglect English. [The author points out that some of the students will attend school outside the reservation and will need to know English.]
>
> K. Hoffman, "Their Native Tongue," *Time for Kids,* 26 January 2001, 4–5.

Student Example: Greg had no trouble with this strategy in his autobiography. In one paragraph he skillfully describes his passion for art and drawing. He begins the next paragraph with, "Although most of my interests are things I like to do alone, there are still a lot of things I like to do in groups and with friends." He goes on to describe his experiences on a soccer team.

Teacher to Teacher   Make sure students understand what the word "although" means and what it signals. If you model a few of these examples of how to use the word "although" to segue from one idea to another, students will catch on to it quickly.

---

7. "Is Another"

In one paragraph, the author makes an assertion and backs up this statement with supporting details. In the next paragraph, he comes back to this assertion and provides additional supporting evidence. He makes the transition from one paragraph to the next by using the words ". . . is another" or "another . . . is."

Example: In the first three paragraphs, the author discusses an aspect of an international meeting on racism. He then goes on to present another issue. He makes the transition to this fourth paragraph from the previous one by using this strategy:

> Another sticky issue was whether countries that took part in slavery should apologize and make payments to the descendants of slaves. Delegates agreed to an apology, but there was no agreement on payments.
>
> "A Struggle to End Prejudice," *Time for Kids,* 7, no. 1, 14 September 2002.

Student Example: Using "Is Another" helps writers stay on track. They focus on one central idea and keep returning to it. Don, a fourth grader, wrote a book report about Ancient Egypt. In his second paragraph, he discusses several ways in which the Nile River contributed to the economy and lifestyle of the Ancient Egyptians. Don begins the third paragraph with "Another use of the Nile River is . . ." He uses this paragraph to describe how the Egyptians drew on the water from the river to grow grapes that were made into wine.

Teacher to Teacher

This strategy is made for "The Lister" (Gillin 2002). "The Lister" is the type of writer who strings together disparate ideas. "Is Another" signals for this writer that he needs to elaborate on each idea. Once he writes "Is another," or "Another . . . is," the writer knows he must devote a paragraph to describing, in detail, the new idea.

8. Appositive

The information that is contained within two commas connects the new ideas to what has preceded them.

Example: Notice how the author of this article uses an appositive in the second paragraph to let the reader know how Mount Myiragongo connects to the context that has already been established. The first two paragraphs read:

> Last week, as rain poured down on scorched earth, people tried to return to their homes in Goma, Democratic Republic of Congo. Many found they had nowhere to go. Their city was buried under a layer of hardened lava.
>
> On January 17, Mount Myiragongo, a volcano near Goma, erupted, sending rivers of red-hot lava into the city . . .
>
> "Congo's Devastating Volcano," *Time for Kids,* 1 February 2002, 2.

Student Example: Young writers don't tend to use appositives, but that's not to say they can't create sentences with them if they are taught how. Luke, a fourth grader, figured out a way to move from one major idea to the next by inserting an appositive. He begins one paragraph by saying, "There are two big cities in Missouri that are part of the east and west regions of Missouri: St. Louis in the east and Kansas City in the west." He continues by describing St. Louis in this paragraph. He starts his next paragraph with, "Kansas City, the other big city in Missouri, is located . . ." He uses the appositive to link this new paragraph back to an idea he began in the preceding one.

Teacher to Teacher   Younger students may need a mini-lesson on what appositives are and how to punctuate them.

9. Several to One

In one paragraph, the author lists several related items. He begins a new paragraph by selecting one item from this list and elaborating on it.

Example: The first paragraph of an article about new state and city leaders provides the reader with a broad statement, announcing that "voters elected state and local leaders." The author then goes from this general statement to the specifics. In the second paragraph, the author talks about Michael Bloomberg's election as mayor of New York City. The following paragraph focuses on the two new Democratic governors from Virginia and New Jersey. The next paragraph zeros in on two cities that picked women mayors for the first time (Atlanta and Cleveland). The final paragraph spotlights Detroit's mayor, Kwame Kilpatrick, one of the country's youngest mayors ("Cities and States Get New Leaders," *Time for Kids*, 16 November 2001, 2).

Student Example: This strategy leads to a very straightforward process. The hardest part is identifying the subtopics. Once you have them, the rest is easy. Maria organized her autobiography with this strategy. She ended one paragraph with, "In the U.S. I've been to New York, New Hampshire, Cape Cod and Pennsylvania." She began the next paragraph by focusing on just one: "Out of all of them New York was my favorite."

Teacher to Teacher | Students may not recognize this strategy on their own and will need help in seeing how this approach is used so often in textbooks. They will then be more adept in applying this strategy in their own writing.

10. Back and Forth

This strategy is used when the author starts with the idea developed in the last paragraph and switches to a new, related idea.

Example: This article explains how genetic engineering has helped farmers by creating corn that produces its own pesticide. Farmers who grow this new kind of corn don't need to rely as heavily on chemical sprays to keep bugs and weeds away. See how the author of this article makes a gentle but effective transition between this idea and a new idea: using genetic engineering to produce vaccines. She begins a new paragraph by connecting back to the idea she just developed and then moving on.

Genetic engineering has mostly helped U.S. farmers. But many scientists are excited about other uses. For example, they are working on ways to put genes that produce vaccines (vak SEENS) into bananas and other foods . . .

N. Fitzgerald, "Food: New and Improved?" National Geographic for Kids!,
November/December 2001, 4–7.

Student Example: Here's where a little creativity comes into play. To have this strategy work, the writer needs to figure out how to make a jump in thinking without losing the reader. Michael, a seventh grader, did a terrific job as he transitioned from one paragraph in which he detailed the dangers of fires to a paragraph in which he identified positive effects of fires. He creates this bridge within the following sentence:

> Forest fires may cause damage but they can also help an ecosystem. First of all, they help clear the bottom of a forest so new plants . . .

Notice how he connects back to the previous paragraph by writing "Forest fires may cause damage" and then moves ahead to a new idea "but they can also help an ecosystem."

Teacher to Teacher This requires the writer to be sophisticated enough to provide a succinct summarizing statement and then slide logically into the new idea.

11. Command

Each new paragraph begins with a verb that moves the reader along from one directive to the next. Words such as "Look," "Check out," "See," and "Take a close look" may be used.

Example: Sylvia Earle, an oceanographer, answers questions about the mysteries of the ocean in this informative interview. When asked, "What's your advice for kids who want to explore the ocean?" she responded by using strong verbs to focus the reader's attention. The first paragraph begins with "Start exploring today." The next paragraph begins, "Look for patterns." Each paragraph includes details that explain more fully how to go about completing each command ("Deep-Sea Diver," *National Geographic for Kids!*, September 2001, 18–21).

Student Example: Barbara has not used this one with her students yet. We've come across several published authors who use it, however, and think it would be valuable to have, especially as students include more graphics in their nonfiction writing.

12. Same Start

The author begins consecutive paragraphs with the same carefully crafted words.

Example: The author uses this strategy to focus on Hazel Barton's range of talents. In the first two paragraphs, the author explains how Hazel Barton loved to be outside and became an expert caver. The third paragraph begins, "Barton also became a scientist." The next (final) paragraph begins with very similar words: "Barton even became a movie star." Each paragraph develops its topic by supplying needed details ("From Science to Screen," *National Geographic for Kids!*, October 2001, 3).

Student Examples: Can this strategy be effective without leading to boring writing? We think it can if it's used carefully. It helped Kara connect a series of studies she found. She began one paragraph with "There have been recent studies . . ." Her next paragraph begins: "There have also been studies . . ."

Theo, a fourth grader, uses this strategy in his report about Virginia. He sets the context for the report in the first two paragraphs and then begins his third paragraph with: "Do you want to know about a famous city in Virginia?" He goes on to tell about Williamsburg. He begins his next paragraph by weaving the word "famous" into the first sentence: "Virginia has some famous people who were born there." Theo uses this paragraph to write about celebrated Virginians: George Washington, Booker T. Washington, and Shirley MacLaine.

Teacher to Teacher   This works well with the more literal writer.

Structures That Connect Ideas Throughout the Entire Text

1. Description

The author paints a picture of one event, one person, one time in history, and the like. All the details in the report clarify and expand this picture.

Example: Readers will walk away with a clear picture of who Catherine Bertini is and the job she does after reading, "A Hero to Hungry Nations." It begins

> Catherine Bertini has 90 million hungry mouths to feed. She had traveled the world as chief of the United Nations World Food Program for nine years. Bertini is responsible for raising money and "making sure food gets to the right people at the right time." [The article continues to describe Catherine Bertini and her role as head of this organization.]
>
> G. Burke, "A Hero to Hungry Nations: She Runs the Biggest Food-Relief Group,"
> *Time for Kids*, 6, no. 20, 9 March 2001, 7.

Student Example: Ken uses this strategy in his fourth-grade report about New Hampshire. The purpose of his report was to describe, in as much detail as possible, what the state of New Hampshire is like. In his opening paragraph he lets the reader know that "New Hampshire is known for its lakes, famous people, and the products it makes."

He begins the next paragraph with, "New Hampshire has many beautiful lakes. New Hampshire's largest lake is . . ." He concludes this paragraph with, "Often people moor their boats in the lakes." The next paragraph begins, "But people have to work in New Hampshire, too."

Ken chooses "Ask a Question" to begin his fourth paragraph: "Do you know any famous people from New Hampshire?" He goes on to talk about Daniel Webster, John Stark, and Franklin Pierce. Did you notice the way Ken transitions from one paragraph to the next? He very effectively uses the "Several to One" strategy described above.

Teacher to Teacher   Although description is a common text structure, it's not always an easy one for students to master. They must know a great deal about their topic, know what's relevant to the purpose of the report, and know how to organize all the details so they are logically arranged.

---

2. Moving Through Time (Sequence)

Each paragraph moves the reader along chronologically. Phrases such as "Five years later," "Not until 1775," or "By the turn of the century" may be used.

Example: You can get a sense of the chronology of events by looking at the signal words used in this article about two young men who left Sudan as refugees and moved to Boston, Massachusetts. The paragraphs begin with words such as "In 1987," "For months," "After three months," "In 1991" (R. Upadhyay, "Sudan's Lost Boys Find a Home," *Time for Kids*, 22 February 2002, 4–5).

Student Example: How can one highlight the complex life of Pablo Picasso in just a few pages? Is this too much to expect from a fifth grader? We may have thought so until we saw how Greg handled it. His carefully placed signal words at the start of several paragraphs helped move the reader along:

> This is why in 1907 . . .
> For the next 30 years, Picasso . . .
> During and after World War II, the main subject of Picasso's paintings . . .

Teacher to Teacher   Brainstorm a list of sequence words before students begin to use this text structure.

---

3. Compare and Contrast

The paragraphs are structured so that the author can identify how topics are similar and different.

Example: Notice how the author contrasts the salaries of men and women who are professional basketball players in this excerpt:

> The average NBA player makes more than $3 million a year. But many women players in the WNBA are getting by with the leagues' minimum yearly salary of $55,000. [The article goes on to highlight what these differences in salaries mean for athletes.]
>
> C. Atticot, "Less for the Ladies?" *Time for Kids*, 6, no. 22, 30 March 2001, 5.

Student Examples: As we mentioned earlier, Barbara's fifth graders liked to use Compare and Contrast as a way to structure their research questions and organize their reports. Elizabeth asked in her lead paragraph, "Do you ever wonder about how figure skating and regular skating are alike and different?" Galen pondered, "I have always wondered what are the differences between falcons that live in cities and those that do not. Are there even differences?"

Teacher to Teacher   Careful planning of data charts prior to the start of the first draft can go a long way in making this organizational structure easy for students to handle.

---

4. Cause and Effect

The author identifies a result (the effect) and what led to this result (the cause).

Example: This article begins with the result and works back to the cause. See if you can determine the cause and effect.

> Get out your red pens! Last week, in a unanimous decision, the Supreme Court ruled that it is legal for students to correct and grade each other's work in class. An Oklahoma mother, Kristja Falvo, had challenged this practice in court.
>
> "Grading by Students Passes a Test," *Time for Kids,* 1 March 2002, 3.

We bet you figured out that what caused the problem was Ms. Falvo's objection to having other students grade her son's work. Her objection led to a court case. The Supreme Court ruled against Ms. Falvo. The decision was the result.

Heather's seventh graders were working on Cause and Effect in their report writing. Several of them introduced their topics in the first paragraph and included in this introduction wording that alerted the reader to the use of the cause-and-effect text structure.

Student Example: Ethan's report focused on the confrontation between Castro and Batista. He gets the reader ready to investigate what led to this conflict and what impact it had on history by writing:

> This event didn't just happen. It was preceded and followed by other events that have causes and effects of their own and the event itself will be a cause of many things to come.

Ethan goes on to elaborate on the relationship of these events in history.

Teacher to Teacher   Making a graphic organizer would be helpful. For example:

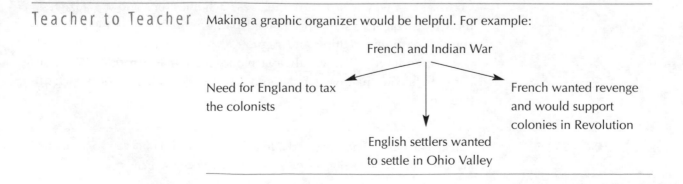

French and Indian War

Need for England to tax the colonists

English settlers wanted to settle in Ohio Valley

French wanted revenge and would support colonies in Revolution

---

5. Explanation

The writer clarifies why something happened or how something works.

Example: Did you ever wonder why white pelicans have such huge pouches under their beaks? The author of "Big Gulp" explains that the pouch helps them catch fish. Excess water that is scooped up along with the fish gets discarded through gaps in its bill when it closes. Pretty interesting, huh? ("Big Gulp," *National Geographic for Kids!,* March 2002, 24).

Student Examples: Quite a few students over the past few years have used this text structure for their reports. Kyle chose it when he explained how a telephone works. Arielle incorporated it in her report about CD-ROMs. Alex demonstrated his knowledge of submarines by explaining clearly how technology is used in modern submarines.

Teacher to Teacher   Suggest that the writer delineate the steps of how something works in a sequential order before writing an explanation.

☑ Checking In with Nick

Let's take another look at Nick's final draft to see how he linked ideas.

Certain to Survive?

(1) It's newborn body weighs only 2 oz., but eventually it will eat about 30 pounds of food each day. Who could eat this much food? An African elephant? A Great White Shark? Nope. The one with the big appetite is the cuddly panda.

(2) You may be wondering where they get all this food. Actually, they eat mostly bamboo, which can be found only in southwest China. It's sad to say that only about 1,000 of them live in the wild and another 100 live in zoos around the world. Why are there so few and what are people doing to protect them?

(3) A long time ago, hunters killed pandas for their fur. It was used for rugs. The pandas had thick fur that kept them warm in their cold weather.

(4) When Pandas were first discovered, they were killed so scientists could study their skin and bones. They were trying to learn more about them. They knew they looked sort of like bears but they didn't hibernate like bears and they can't walk on their hind legs. Also, pandas can grab

onto bamboo easily because one of their bones in their wrists is larger and longer than the others. They also have strong jaws and strong teeth witch helps them eat the hard bamboo. If you was a scientist wouldn't you want to find out about all these unique things about pandas too?

(5) Another reason there are so few pandas is because people have built homes and farms in the mountain valleys of China where pandas used to live. The pandas had to move up into the colder mountains to get food and water. This was not good because they ran out of their food supply and because they had to live closer to men who could kill them.

(6) Today the Chinese government is protecting pandas and their land. It's now against the law to kill them and officials plant bamboo so pandas always have enough food.

(7) Although man has killed lots of pandas in the past now people everywhere want to help pandas. Pandas have been brought to zoos where zookeepers give them vitamins and put them on special diets to keep them healthy. Sometimes they live in dark, air-conditioned sections of the zoo, so they feel like they are at home in the mountains of China. Pandas like to be near water, so zookeepers make sure they have plenty to use for drinking, playing and cooling off. Pandas who live in the wild usually live about 15 years. Pandas who live in captivity can live into their 20s.

(8) No matter if the pandas live in China or in a zoo, it seems that everyone is now working hard to make sure they live long, safe lives. Perhaps this will help keep pandas from becoming extinct so people in years to come can also enjoy these cuddly-looking animals.

You'll notice that Nick has organized his report around an explanation text structure, but within this structure he also organizes his notes sequentially by time. He connects the first and second paragraphs by holding on to the idea of "food." He ends the second paragraph with his research question. It's at the start of the third paragraph that he moves into the time sequence: "A long time ago . . ."

In the fourth paragraph, see how he takes the reader back in time "When pandas were first discovered . . ." In this paragraph he develops more of his explanation of why the number of pandas is declining by giving another reason and supporting it. He nicely transitions to the fifth paragraph by using the "Is Another" strategy.

At the start of the following paragraph (6), Nick brings us to the current time: "Today the Chinese government . . ." It's in this paragraph that he begins to answer the second part of his research question: What's being done to protect them?

He moves to paragraph 7 by using the "Although" strategy. He contrasts what used to happen to pandas and what is being done now to keep them safe. Nick connects to the final paragraph by using Repeat a Word (He repeats the word "live").

Nick's trying hard to build cohesiveness into his report. The paper is much more connected than his first draft. It was quite a challenge for Nick to juggle all the pieces so "their ideas" could become "his ideas" and now "our ideas." The best part is that he now has the tools he needs to be able to go through this process independently.

What's Next?

As we mentioned earlier, we need to return to the leads. We'll start with the lead Nick wrote on his first report: "I am doing a report on the panda bear." We'll introduce Nick to strategies he can try to make this introduction more inviting. We're convinced that once he knows how to write better leads, he'll hook his readers with his first sentence.

It Started How? Leads

*Good leads set up expectations in the reader's mind and also, like
flashlights, they help writers to see where they are heading.*
—Barry Lane, *After the End*

We've all been at a school when the recess bell rings and children
try to outdo each other to secure the coveted first place in line.
You may observe a number of tactics: some children spend their
entire recess hanging around the entrance to the building, some run people
down to get to the head of the line, and some engage in play but edge closer
and closer to the door as the recess period winds down. One morning, Mary
asked some third graders why this phenomenon takes place. A perceptive
student responded, "The leader's job is to get everyone where they need to
go." The leader plays an important role. He is the immediate focus of attention. He sets the standard for the other students to follow.

In a sense, the role of the class leader is very similar to the role of the lead
sentence or sentences in a report. The lead serves several purposes. It

1. piques the reader's interest;
2. sets expectations for what is to come;
3. provides a focus; and
4. engages the reader in the text.

Most writers struggle with leads. They understand that leads are important. They either hook the reader into the piece or turn the reader away.
Lukeman (2000) brings this "hook" analogy to life. He states, "If you barely
hook a fish, say, by the edge of his lip, there is a chance he'll get away. But if

you hook him deeply, say, through his entire cheek, he is yours" (p. 153). This graphic comparison clearly illustrates how important the lead is. Silverman, Hughes, and Wienbroer (1999) also emphasize the significance of this first exchange between the reader and writer. They note that all beginnings and endings in life demand special attention. Think about the time and effort that goes into planning a wedding. We want everything to be perfect for the new bride and groom. Think back to your first day of school (or the first day of school for one of your own children). How did you get ready? Do you remember how you prepared for your first day on your first job? We remember being up all night making sure everything was just so. All these new beginnings are important. It takes a great deal of thinking and time to prepare for new beginnings. We need to acknowledge this when writing leads. They don't just happen.

Knowing this, some writers place undue pressure on themselves by expecting the lead to be exemplary on the first try. This type of writer may sit forever staring at the blank page, waiting for the perfect lead to strike. Other writers have only one strategy in their repertoire of leads. They begin each piece using the same strategy, regardless of the topic, audience, or text structure. For example, one strategy young authors often rely on begins with the word "I" and contains the topic of the paper—no more, no less. You may recognize some of these leads:

"I have been asked to write about [topic]."
"I will tell you about [topic]."
"I am writing about [topic]."

Although not engaging, these leads can be very useful. They provide the writer with confidence and something on which to build; there is no longer a blank page. They also help students focus on the topic. While the thesis statement in these leads is obvious and clear, students need to be taught how to move beyond this one, safe type of lead.

Leading Off

It's common to hear teachers say, "Just put something down. Write anything just to get started." We've said this ourselves. However, this is not always as easy to do as it sounds, especially if we don't want to write a "My report is about . . ." type of lead. As we explained in the introduction to Part 2, we were at a loss when it came to teaching students about leads. The two of us had written hundreds of leads; yet we struggled to convey our practices to the students. Looking inward didn't help us, so we turned to children's nonfiction magazines for assistance. We scoured our school and local libraries looking at *Boys' Life, Kids Discover, Cobblestone, Animals, Odyssey,* and other similar publications in search of leads that grabbed our attention. Each of us found dozens of interesting leads to share as examples, so we thought we were home free. We soon discovered, however, that reading/showing the leads to the students wasn't enough; we had to unlock how the author put together words to create each of these attention grabbers. By discussing the effect each lead had on us as readers and determining how the author achieved this effect, we gradually put together a collection of leads and strategies to share with students. You'll find these later in this chapter.

Caution!

Before we begin, it might be helpful to think about what to avoid when writing leads or teaching others to write leads. Knowing what leads *are not* may be as beneficial as knowing what they *are*.

We bet you can think of at least one student who has carefully planned a great hook—maybe it shocks the reader into reading more; perhaps it contains a lovely metaphor; or it might end with an intriguing question. As the reader, you're eager to continue reading. Slowly you realize that the lead has nothing to do with the body of the paper. There is a total disconnect. Lukeman (2000) cautions, "The current popular misconception is that hooks are synonymous with marketing gimmicks," which often leads "to discrepancies between hooks and the body of the text" (p. 155). Since the lead sets up the reader for what's to come, it's important that writers not only draft an interesting hook but one that logically brings the reader into the remainder of the paper.

Roth (1989) shares some other things to avoid when writing leads. You can probably add on to her list and adjust it to meet the needs of students with whom you work. Roth suggests the following:

> Don't repeat the title in the first paragraph.
> Don't tell what the purpose of the paper will be. Simply do what you propose to do. Stating what you'll do may make the reader impatient and shows a lack of imagination.
> Don't give a dictionary definition in the lead.
> Don't write a cute or folksy opening. (pp. 170–171)

We're not suggesting that you necessarily abide by Roth's guidelines. We are suggesting, however, that it's important for teachers to share their thinking with their students. Let students know your expectations. Perhaps you could involve your students in designing a group "Things to Avoid" list (Roth 1989).

No matter how you introduce the strategies, it is important to note Lane's (1993) advice: "Leads are not introductions writers nail on at the beginning of their pieces; they are seeds writers plant. Because different plants grow from different seeds, writers must search for the right lead" (p. 18).

The following fifteen strategies may help students in this search for the right lead. Although they are arranged from Beginning to Mastering to Advanced (see Figure 5.1), these levels do not represent a clear hierarchy and should be approached accordingly. It's best to go slowly and model only a few strategies at one time. It's been helpful for us to know as much about each student's research question as possible so we can match writer and strategy. We are then able to group students to teach effective strategies.

Figure 5.1 Lead Strategies

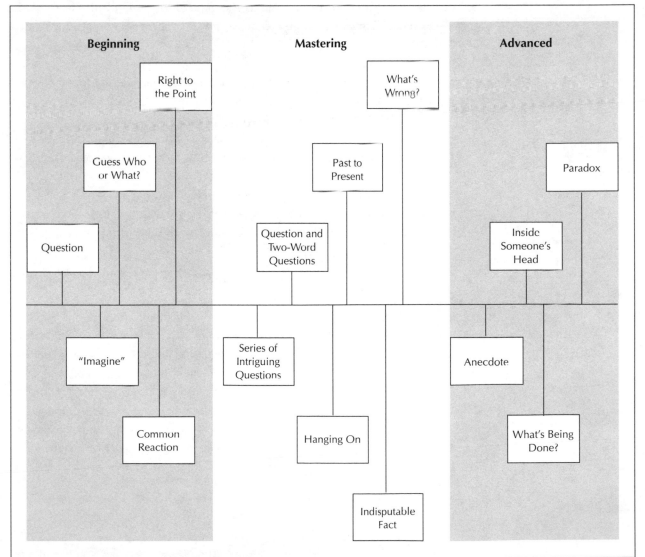

Beginning Strategies

Beginning strategies are effective in many situations and are fairly easy for students to implement.

1. Question

The author begins the report by posing a thought-provoking, open-ended question. This question serves two purposes: it introduces the topic and encourages the reader to read on to discover the answer.

Example: Watch how the author of "Time to Change Election Rules?" gets the reader ready for this article by posing the following question: "Do millionaires, big businesses, unions and rich organizations have too much influence in U.S. elections?" ("Time to Change Election Rules?" *Time for Kids*, 6, no. 23, 6 April 2001, 2).

Student Examples: Kyle, Mai, and Maria ask the following questions to invite readers into their reports on the telephone, Beethoven, and Pluto, respectively:

> Have you ever wondered how you talk to your best friend or a family member just by picking up something called a phone and dialing seven numbers?
>
> Have you ever heard of a composer that was deaf?
>
> Have you ever wanted to solve one of the greatest mysteries in the world? [Maria goes on to debate whether Pluto is a planet or comet.]

Teacher to Teacher   Most students seem to like this strategy. It gives them a quick, direct way into the report. This strategy, however, is not as easy to use as it may appear. The question needs to be intriguing. It needs to provoke some reaction in the reader. It needs to set realistic expectations for the scope and depth of the report. It needs to engage the reader's curiosity in order to be effective. Students need to understand these connections.

In some cases, students pose an interesting question and then proceed to answer the question in the same paragraph. Unfortunately, in these instances, there is nothing left to say in the remainder of the report. Teachers may want to caution writers about asking a question and summarizing the answer in the same paragraph.

2. "Imagine"

The author hooks the reader by drawing him directly into a scene that evokes another time, place, or situation. The word "imagine" often occurs in this lead.

Example: Notice how this lead catches the reader's attention.

> Imagine growing up without puzzles, a Playstation or a Poo-Chi. [The article goes on to tell how some children create their own toys because they either live in places where there are no toy stores or because they are too poor to afford toys.]
>
> "Priceless Toys," *Time for Kids*, 27 April 2001, 6.

Student Examples: Kathryn brings us back in time as she introduces how the world might have begun, while Arielle, her classmate, takes her readers on a mysterious journey as she applies this strategy in her report about CD-ROMs:

> *Kathryn:* Imagine you are way, way, way, way back in time, before people, before dinosaurs, before the earth and stars, even before the universe. You are in a cloud of nothing. It is so very hot, especially near this fireball of some sort. You don't know what it is or what it is going to do, and all of a sudden, BANG!

> *Arielle:* Imagine you are in a long hallway. You can't see the beginning or the end. The hallway is miles long. You look up. Someone has put a pattern of bathtubs and mirrors upside down on the ceiling. As far as you can see, there are bathtubs and mirrors . . .

Teacher to Teacher   Students enjoy this strategy because of their vivid imaginations and their ability to be creative. It works for most topics because it's so open-ended. Students may need to be reminded that they are responsible for setting up expectations that are relevant to the rest of the report and that don't mislead the reader. They must be able to connect their imagery back to the topic in meaningful ways.

3. Guess Who or What?

The author immediately snatches the reader's attention by inviting him to solve a riddle.

Example: Can you tell what the author of "A Really Bad Hair Day" is describing?

Guess who's hiding behind the hairdo. Here are some clues. It's an animal that can survive for weeks without a drop to drink. (You couldn't survive beyond a few days without water.) This shaggy animal is healthy and comfortable with a body temperature anywhere from 93 [degrees] F to 104 [degrees] F. (Your normal temperature is 98.6 [degrees] F. If it varies more than a couple of degrees up or down, you probably don't feel well.) Still don't know? The animal can plod steadily across 30 miles of parched desert in a day carrying more than 300 pounds on its back. (Could you walk 30 miles in a day even without a load?) If you're still unsure about the creature behind the hair, take an upside-down peek at the answer below.

This animal is a Bactrian camel. It has two humps on its back.

D. G. Gordon, "A Really Bad Hair Day," *National Geographic World*, May 2000, 3.

Student Example: Sarah enjoyed writing riddles and asking questions. Can you figure out what she researched?

Here is a riddle. What has three parts, has plants and trees living on it like you and me, and is very, very, very large? Give up? It is the Earth.

Sarah then goes on to highlight some facts in a question-and-answer format:

Did you ever wonder about how much of the world is water and how much is dry land? The Earth is about 70 percent water and only 30 percent land. Have you ever wondered what would happen if the ozone layer disappeared? You should because if the ozone layer was gone the sun might vaporize all the water on the Earth, leaving it very dry. Have you ever wondered why the temperature of the Earth is so comfortable? It is so comfortable because we are not too close to the sun or too far. The first part of the Earth is very, very hot, and if it was possible for a person to be there, they would burn up instantly. The core is the name of this extremely hot place. It is made up of two parts, the inner core and the outer core. Both are made up of two metals: nickel and iron. Nothing lives in the core.

Originally, Sarah used this lead to introduce her report:

The earth is about 4.6 billion years old. It weighs about 6,000,000,000,000,000,000,000 [lbs.]. That number is 6 million trillions. The radius of the earth is about 3,950 miles. Also, the shape of the earth is a sphere. [Sarah continues with thirteen more sentences of random facts.]

Be careful that the writer does not give too much information away.

4. Common Reaction

With this strategy, the author begins with a generally held impression of her topic.

Example: Who can help but feel the pain from the Columbine shootings? The hurt that has stung the nation still continues. This article urges the reader to examine the issue of gun violence in the United States.

> It still hurts. The shootings one year ago at Columbine High School in Littleton, Colorado, have left a painful dark mark on the nation, like a bad bruise that is slow to fade. It hurts to think of the two teenage gunmen and the 15 lives they took. It hurts to think that anything like it could ever happen again.
>
> M. Tauber, "The Gun Debate," *Time for Kids*, 5, no. 24, 21 April 2002.

Student Examples: Chad wanted to make sure everyone knows what it's like on Mercury. Here's how he hooked his readers. "It's SOOOOOO steaming hot. That's what people would think when they see Mercury."

We encourage writers to write from experience, and that's exactly what Vanessa did when she tried this strategy to kick off her autobiography. She began "It's sooooo hard!" and went on to describe what it's like to begin taking dance lessons.

This strategy often works with animal reports or with any other topic that might evoke strong feelings.

5. Right to the Point

The author begins with one short, clear, declarative sentence that states the main idea. The curt statement begs for a fuller explanation, which is found in the remainder of the report.

Example: The author begins this article about President Bush with the following simple but attention-grabbing sentence: "New Presidents like to act fast" (K. Hoffman, "Down to Business," *Time for Kids*, 6, no. 16, 2 February 2001, 6).

Chapter 5: It Started How?

Student Example: Michael demonstrates that he understands this strategy by using it to introduce his report on computers:

> Many parts make up the computer. The video card translates instruction into a computer. An expansion card lets you add a new feature on a computer. The computer also holds a sound card which determines the quality of sound produced.

Teacher to Teacher   You may want to encourage students to try this strategy when responding to prompts on standardized tests. You might begin by asking the writer what the main point is in order to help him focus on the relevant idea. With Right to the Point, the writer identifies the main point of the essay/report and places it firmly in the first sentence. Test scorers don't have to hunt for the topic sentence and students don't lose sight of what the prompt is asking. Unlike "I have been asked to write about . . .," however, this lead raises questions in the reader's mind, which impels him to read on.

Mastering Strategies

The strategies below may be suitable for students who have an in-depth understanding of their topics and a broad range of writing skills. The first two are sophisticated variations of the Question strategy (see No. 1 above).

6. Series of Intriguing Questions

The writer provides a series of well-designed, open-ended questions that may appear to be unconnected. The questions urge the reader on, setting up the expectation that the questions will be answered and that the relationship that ties them together will be revealed.

Example: See how cleverly the author used this strategy to keep the reader wondering where he was going in the following lead:

> What's it like to be a kangaroo with a gangly joey, arms and legs all akimbo, riding in your front pouch like a curious human infant bent on leaping from his carriage? Or how about a Laysan duck running through a swarm of flies with its beak agape to catch a bit of dinner? Or one wildebeest in a frenzied, migrating throng hoping to avoid the Nile crocodiles stationed at a river crossing?

Mitsuaki Iwago and his camera want to know . . .

J. Praded, "Where Magic and Reality Mix: Book Review," *Animals,*
May/June 1999, 8–11.

Student Example: Galen used a slight variation of this strategy as the lead for his autobiography:

> What's green, swims, and hops around? A frog!! What has feathers, flies and has a beak? A bird!!! What is freckled, has red hair, and plays soccer? ME!!! What is this person that plays soccer, has red hair, and has freckles like?

Teacher to Teacher This strategy is more challenging than Questions because in order to use it effectively, the writer must ask multiple open-ended questions that tease the reader into wondering what links them together. When students begin to experiment with this strategy they sometimes list a series of literal questions such as "Is Pluto a comet or a planet? Is it far away? How large is it?" They may conclude with: "In this report, you will find out." The purpose of this strategy isn't to simply pose questions about a topic, it is to whet the reader's appetite for the topic. Each question must be intriguing and should heighten the reader's curiosity.

In other cases, students may ask questions that are captivating but that do not relate specifically to the thesis. In either case, modeling and discussion help to clarify this strategy.

---

7. Question and Two-Word Questions

The author begins by asking one major question and then breaks this question down into a series of two-word subquestions.

Student Example: Chloe, a fifth grader, came up with this strategy. We think it really helps focus the reader's attention on the key elements of her report. Would you agree?

> Did you ever wonder what it would be like to live in Japan? What are the schools like? The homes? The traditions? Japan is a very fascinating place.

Originally, Chloe's report began:

> Did you ever wonder what it would be like to be in Japan? Well, I did. My report will tell you what it would be like to live in Japan. I researched their schools, their traditional houses, their traditions, and

found some interesting facts about Japan. Japan is a very fascinating place.

While the content of the two leads remained consistent, the revised lead is much more engaging than Chloe's first attempt. Rather than telling the reader what is to come, the series of questions subtly guides the reader to realize that the report will address these areas. We couldn't find examples of this strategy in children's magazines, but we think it has great potential.

Teacher to Teacher

This strategy will not work for every report. The report must have two or three specific subcategories that are going to be investigated. The organization of the data chart into subtopics will naturally take the writer along this route. Michael, who used Right to the Point, could have chosen this strategy to begin his report. He could have begun: "Did you ever wonder how a computer works? What does the video card do? The expansion card? The sound card?

8. Hanging On

The author provides a series of clues, which the reader uses to uncover the identity of the topic.

Example: Isn't this an ingenious way to keep the reader hanging on? What could this author be describing?

> Its body stretched flat in the water, the hunter swims toward the prey. One hop, and the hunter is out of the water, snatching its catch. Licking its lips, it prepares to devour its meal.
>
> A ruthless killer? An unlucky victim? Nope. The hunter is a fluffy muskrat, looking more like a bedroom slipper than a dangerous predator. Its prey is an apple slice, hidden in an exhibit at the Museum of Life and Science in Durham, NC.
>
> D. A. Bailey, "Call of the Wild," *Boys' Life,* July 1999, 14.

Rather than coming right out and saying that this article is about a fluffy muskrat, the author keeps the reader hanging on, leading her to wonder what is being written about.

Student Example: Galen, a fifth grader, cleverly holds the reader spellbound by using this strategy. See how he integrates information from the "Interesting Facts" column on his data chart into this lead. How does this affect the quality of his writing?

It flies silently high in the air and circles looking for prey. It sights a mouse in the grass. It dives at a speed that could be over 200 miles per hour. It grabs the mouse with its talons then severs the mouse's spinal cord with its beak. Still haven't guessed? It is a bird of prey. It's smaller than a hawk. It lives in some of the world's largest cities and some of the most rural areas. The answer is a falcon.

Through this clever lead, Galen has introduced us to his research topic. In the next paragraph, he identifies the thesis of his report.

I have always wondered what are the differences between falcons that live in cities and those that do not. Are there even differences? Through research I found out there are many differences and interesting facts about falcons. What lets a falcon live around people and what lets them not live around people?

Teacher to Teacher · With this strategy, the writer needs to balance the amount of accurate information he reveals with a level of evasiveness so the reader can draw his own conclusions. This became one of the most popular strategies, as it encourages students to showcase their creativity. You can probably imagine why. Don't hesitate to try this one out. Why not model a few examples and have some fun yourself?

---

9. Past to Present

The author makes a connection with the past. He notes how things once were and then moves to the present.

Example: Wouldn't it be fun to know more about Cleopatra and the city in which she lived? Well, archaeologists have found the lost city. The article begins,

More than 1,600 years ago, a flourishing royal court full of treasures was swallowed up by the sea. The island of Antirhodos (An-teer-uh-dose), home of Cleopatra, the famous queen of Egypt, sank after the area was hit by a huge earthquake in A.D. 335.

The next paragraph jumps to current times.

In 1996, French explorer Franck Goddio rediscovered this fabled city. [Notice how the author identified two specific years (A.D. 335 and 1996) to move the reader through time.]

R. Upadhyay, "Cleopatra's Lost City," *Time for Kids,* 20 April 2001, 6.

Student Example: Danny tried out several strategies but decided on the Past to Present strategy. It was a perfect choice for his report about automobiles:

> If you lived more than a hundred years ago you'd probably be wondering what horse you would be riding to school. By the 1900s, though, a new invention, the automobile, was created.

Danny's report is about how automobiles have changed over the past one hundred years. His original report began with

> Automobiles are about 100 years old. They have changed a lot over the years. This is an interesting subject for me. I have found many changes in automobiles.

Instead of just stating the fact that automobiles are one hundred years old, Danny set this fact in an interesting context. Danny decided to bring the reader back in time to illustrate what it would have been like to live then. This is a good example of "showing" rather than "telling." Danny could have told us "If you lived 100 years ago, you'd be riding a horse to school." Instead, however, he gently leads the reader to draw this conclusion for himself. Next, Danny transitions us to the 1900s with word "though."

Teacher to Teacher Again, each student needs to discern whether or not this strategy is appropriate for her topic. In many cases it's useful to situate the topic in an historical perspective, but the nature and purpose of the report will often dictate whether this is an apt decision.

---

10. Indisputable Fact

The writer leads off with a statement that is unquestionable; one with which everyone could agree.

Example: This strategy is displayed in a brief biographical sketch of Sojourner Truth:

> Sojourner Truth was born into slavery in 1797 in New York. At birth, she was named Isabella Baumfree. She had many owners who treated her badly.
>
> "Freedom Fighter: Sojourner Truth," *Time for Kids*, 22 February 2002, 3.

Student Example: Wouldn't it be wonderful if every child could start an autobiography the way Sarah did: "In my life, I have people who care about me and love me"?

The simplicity of an indisputable-fact statement catches the reader's attention. In some ways it is similar to Right to the Point. However, unlike Right to the Point, the first sentence sets forth an assertion that is irrefutable and unquestionable.

11. What's Wrong?

There is a problem. The author clearly identifies it in the lead sentence.

Example: What could be the problem with cuddly sea otters? The author of this article identifies a serious concern.

> Sea otters that live off the coast of Alaska's Aleutian Islands are in trouble. Recently the U.S. Fish and Wildlife Service counted only 6,000 of these furry little mammals living along the 1,000-mile stretch of the islands. In the 1980s, the sea otter population was estimated at 50,000 to 100,000.
>
> "Sea Otters Take a Dip," *National Geographic for Kids*, September 2001, 2.

The article goes on to explain environmental problems that may cause this dwindling number of sea otters.

Student Examples: Krystal tried this strategy to begin her report on water pollution:

> In the world many people pollute the water. When people throw trash in rivers, oceans, or lakes, it is polluting the water. Also, factories sometimes turn waterways into open sewers by dumping oils, toxic chemicals, and other harmful industrial wastes into bodies of water. People pollute the water every day and it's bad for the environment.

Julia identifies the problem in her report on housing in China: "China needs houses!" Her report, based on an interview with a relative who spent time in China, documents what the housing situation is like and why there should be more available housing.

Teacher to Teacher   Similar to Right to the Point, this strategy states the gist of the report in the first sentence. Unlike the former strategy, however, What's Wrong? is appropriate to use only if there is a problem that's being addressed. The author must identify the key point of the problem, which makes this slightly more challenging than merely stating a fact, as is the case with Right to the Point.

These strategies are the most sophisticated, requiring abstract thinking and an understanding of the complexity of language.

12. Anecdote

The writer shares a short story that relates to the report's topic.

Example: This piece, "Allure of the Weasel," begins more like fiction than nonfiction. We're introduced to ferrets through an incident that happened to the ferret's owner.

> Ann Rudich laughs when she recalls the time she arrived home from work to find her ferret, Jagger, lying exhausted in the middle of a huge pile of socks and pantyhose. He had spent the day collecting clothing from the laundry room and from every dresser drawer. "Jagger rolls over, begs, and fetches. His biggest problem is, he loves socks," says Rudich, who lives in Shrewsbury, Massachusetts.
>
> P. H. Sacks, "Allure of the Weasel," *Animals*, January/February 2000, 14–17.

Student Examples: Professional writers employ this strategy in biographies, but it's an extremely difficult one for students. The writer needs to relay a personal memory, which resources don't often contain. Bobby, a fifth grader in a school near Barbara's, however, caught our attention when he began his report on Colin Powell with an anecdote. His teacher had been modeling this strategy with them, and it paid off for Bobby.

> One day in 1963 when Colin Powell was walking through [a] rice paddy, he stepped in a trap. As his foot touched the trap, a sharp stake shot through the bottom of his foot. When his foot was cured, he received a Purple Heart.

We shared this strategy with Heather. Was it as effective for her seventh graders? After reading the introductions that Nancy and Janice wrote, you decide.

> *Nancy*: It is very dark. Walking through the night in a thick black forest, suddenly the Costa Rican border is just ahead. You can see it perfectly. The lights are in a near row. It comforts you to think that you are finally there. The very long, tiring journey from Colombia is finally over. A sudden relief swarms over your body like ants over a breadcrumb on a

hot summer day. Then you think to yourself, "Wait a minute. Lights? Out in the middle of nowhere? How can that be?" Then you realize the only thing keeping you from crossing the border. A hard lump forms in your throat. The guards are standing everywhere. They are as omnipresent as the forest and the air that is surrounding you. Now the only task left is to get past those guards. But how? Shivers run up and down your spine like a mouse escaping danger with its reward, the cheese, clamped tightly in its mouth. You freeze, thinking. You start to panic. "What do I do?!?! Oh what am I going to do?!?! Where do I go from here?!?!

Janice: His aging eyes glistened with anticipation. Francois Duvalier awoke to his first day as Haiti's president. The morning was colorful, as if a giant paintbrush had swept through the sky. Duvalier stood upon his cold balcony overlooking the country that was now his. Far off in the distance, he could see the ocean sparkling and the Haitians just awaking and slowly trudging themselves to school and work. The smell of eggs and bacon made its way up Duvalier's nostrils and filled him with anxiousness for the up coming years of his presidency. The Haitian's past history had been tumultuous and leaderless, all of the Haitians needed a good leader, and Duvalier intended to fill that void. The Duvalier legacy was bound to have mistakes, just like every other event, it too has causes and effects.

These anecdotes are enjoyable to read. We can't help but think that the students had fun writing them, too. There is so much voice and passion embedded in them (and wonderful similes, too!). Their knowledge base is clearly evident in these leads.

Teacher to Teacher   Although this can be a truly effective strategy, there are many factors to consider.
- First, the students must know a great deal about their topics in order to use this strategy.
- Second, the anecdote must relate closely to the topic of the report.
- Third, the tone of the anecdote should correspond to the tone of the report. If you are asking students to write a formal report, an informal anecdote will not be appropriate. On the other hand, if the report is informal, an anecdote may be just the strategy to use.
- Fourth, the anecdote must be brief.
- Fifth, the anecdotal sketch must not lead the reader astray; it must set up expectations that materialize in the remainder of the report.

---

13. Inside Someone's Head

With this strategy, the author reveals what someone or something is thinking.

Example: We get a sense of what sports writer Jane Gottesman was thinking and feeling during the 1994 Winter Olympics as she recalls her thoughts in this short excerpt. Notice how the words "Gottesman remembers" help the reader know he's catching a glimpse of what's going on inside her head.

> Jane Gottesman will never forget how she felt when she opened the sports section of her newspaper during the 1994 Winter Olympics. She read that both Picabo (PEEK-uh-boo) Street and Alberto Tomba had won silver medals in skiing. "There was a photograph of Street with a cowboy hat on, smiling her big Picabo smile," Gottesman remembers. "And there was a photo of Alberto Tomba, racing. Tomba looked like an athlete. Street didn't. That really bothered me."
>
> S. Macy, "Putting Women in the Picture," *National Geographic for Kids!*,
> January/February 2002, 10–13.

Student Example: Nobody really knows what's inside someone else's head, but Luke has fun with this strategy when he pretends to know what crops might be thinking:

> "It has perfect weather for me except for the tornadoes." That is what the crops of Missouri would say if they could talk.

Luke's use of Inside Someone's Head caught his reader off guard, but it certainly was effective in getting his main point across.

Teacher to Teacher | This is like stream of consciousness with a focus, while inside someone else's head! Have fun with it.

---

14. What's Being Done

The lead immediately introduces the reader to the issue at hand and the step(s) taken to address the issue.

Examples: The author of this article clearly acknowledges the need to protect Asian and American bears:

> Senator Mitch McConnell, a Kentucky Republican, has promised to reintroduce a bill in the U.S. Senate to help stem the poaching of both

Asian and American bears. If passed, the Bear Protection Act would ban the sale of a bear's internal organs, such as the gall bladder, used in traditional Asian medicine . . .

"NewsScan," *Animals*, May/June 1999, 6.

Similarly, the reader immediately knows not only what's wrong but also what's being done in this lead about the animal:

In an effort to draw attention to the struggles of Australia's koala, the U.S. Fish and Wildlife Service (USFWS) is seeking to have the animal listed as threatened under the Endangered Species Act (ESA).

S. Sawicki, "NewsScan," *Animals*, January/February 1999, 6–7.

Student Example: Is this an easy strategy to use? No, but Joy, a seventh grader, did a terrific job of giving all the essential facts in the lead paragraph of her report on media violence. At the same time, she refrains from giving away the entire report in this opener:

Over the past few years, there have been millions and millions of violent acts on television. There have also been millions and millions of kids who have watched them. Some people believe that it has influenced the way children think and act around others . . . After learning this information [results from her survey of parents], media violence has an effect on children, but there are ways that parents and other people can help. [Joy goes on to explain how people can "limit the effect of media violence on children."]

Teacher to Teacher   This strategy works well with topics that need action, such as endangered animals, preservation of historical places, or health issues.

---

15. Paradox (Something That Goes Against Common Sense)

With this strategy, there appears to be a contradiction between what has been written and what we believe to be true.

Example: The lead into this article really catches the reader's attention. Does this seem believable to you?

Little Red Riding Hood would be shocked. Wolves have returned to Yellowstone National Park, and many Americans are thrilled. [The article goes on to explain that many people see the wolf as a beautiful, endangered species that should be protected.]

"Big, Back Wolf," *National Geographic for Kids!*, January/February 2002, 3.

Student Example: Even with several examples, this strategy may be a challenge for some upper elementary and middle school students. Not so for Greg, however, a fifth grader who wrote a report that explained why Pablo Picasso had so many styles and periods. He led into his report by asking two questions that seem to be inconsistent with what one would expect:

> Did you know that two toy cars and a broken pitcher could be considered a great work of art? And that a faucet and an old shovel could be considered a masterpiece? Out of the cars and pitcher, Pablo Picasso made a baboon. Out of the faucet and shovel, Picasso made a crane. [Greg goes on to say that Picasso was one of the world's greatest artists and that he went through many different styles and periods, which the report investigates.]

Teacher to Teacher

This strategy is appropriate for students who have a passion for their topic and are ready for a challenge. They need to be able to play with language and complex ideas.

Blending Strategies

Some students may decide to blend two or more of the strategies to produce interesting leads. Iris, for example, uses Imagine and Question to create a very inviting lead for her jaguar report:

> Try to imagine that you are on a trip in South America. You are on a tour of a Brazilian rain forest and you see a spotted animal and a black animal. You think the spotted animal is a jaguar but you're not sure. Can you guess what kind of animal the black one is? Well, as you might have guessed, the black animal is not a black panther. But it is a female jaguar. Female jaguars are usually always black. In fact, a jaguar cub usually will have a black mother and a spotted father.

Writers should understand that there are endless options available to them when creating leads. They should be encouraged to have fun, take risks, and see what works (and perhaps what doesn't).

☑ Checking In with Nick

Throughout the book, we have been following Nick, who has been researching panda bears and writing his report based on information from several sources. Today we find Nick revising his lead. He has decided to try out one strategy from each level. In addition, he attempted to combine two strategies to create a hook for his report.

Using Lead Strategies to Revise Nick's Panda Report

You may recall Nick's original lead:

> I am doing a report on the panda bear. I picked the panda bear because it is cute and cuddly. I hope you enjoy reading my report and learning about this animal.

You'll see that Nick has come a long way when you read some of the revised leads he's written. Which one of these leads do you think he should use, or should he continue to experiment with other strategies?

> Beginning—*Common Reaction:* "They're soooo ADORABLE. That's how most people react to panda bears."
>
> Mastering—*Indisputable Fact:* "Pandas are black and white mammals that are related to raccoons."
>
> Advanced—*Paradox:* "Panda bears are not bears."
>
> Combination of strategies—*What's Being Done* and *Question:* "Unless man wakes up and recognizes the dangers pandas are facing, there will no longer be any left in the wild. Wouldn't that be a shame?"

What's Next?

Nick is getting there. He has a rough draft that is well organized and a stronger lead than he did before. His paper is still lacks a sense of closure, however. In the next chapter, we'll turn our attention to ways in which we can help students write conclusions that signal for their readers that a logical ending is approaching.

Is It Done Yet?
Conclusions

Conclusions should "knock the people's socks off."
—Dominick, a fourth grader

How many times have we seen "The End" scrawled across the bottom of a student's paper? It seems that the more white space there is on the last page, the larger these two little words become. Some students express their own personalities in how they design "The End." They add color, or swirls; some enclose the words in boxes or clouds. What these students may not know is that if they did a good job of concluding their pieces, they wouldn't need to write these words at all. The reader would know that he had reached the end. There would be closure.

Writing an effective conclusion is much more difficult than ending a person-to-person conversation, where body language can help bring closure. Written language has to be much more intentional and planned. The writer can't reach out and hug the reader while quickly adding, "Give me a call" as she runs off. She needs to prepare the reader gradually for the ending. This happens from the very start of the piece. If done well, the conclusion fits in with and extends what has come before it. The writing continually snowballs in a logical way. One idea advances to the next, from the lead sentence to the final word. Strong conclusions never materialize abruptly, they never appear as add-ons, and they never introduce something that has not already been developed in the body of the paper.

Writers can craft conclusions in many ways, but often less experienced writers find one way to end their papers and conclude everything they write in the same way. They may routinely bring closure to papers by saying, "Now you know about . . . [topic]," or "I have told you all about . . . [topic]," or "I hope you have learned about . . . [topic]," or "I hope you liked my report on . . . [topic]," or "If you want to find out more, go to the library or the Internet." Often these endings just appear. They are tacked on to what precedes them. They serve the purpose of finishing off the piece, but they fall flat and leave the reader disappointed. Why do students continue to rely on these perfunctory conclusions? It may be because students are not sure when they're done.

Whether we're working with third graders or graduate students, a popular question is "How many pages does it have to be?" Our standard answer, and probably yours, too, is "As long as it takes to get the job done." But when is the job done? This is a tough question, especially for beginning researchers. A good rule of thumb to follow is that a writer knows she's done when she has answered her research question and the same set of answers begins to show up in all the resources. She is not uncovering any new information. Then it's pretty safe to say she's done. It's so important to spend time doing the preliminary reading prior to determining the focus of research. The reading provides the researcher with a sense of how broad the topic is. Formulating the research question is also important because it can limit or expand your inquiry. Depending on the big question or thesis statement, "done" may be a few sentences or volumes.

"Done" may sneak up on writers. A teacher may give the students a set length for the paper: "Your report should be three to four double-spaced pages long." Or "This assignment should contain between 750 and 1,000 words." A student collects information, writes the report, and finds that before he realizes it, he has reached the required number of pages or words for the assignment. He thinks, "Wow! I'm done." So he wraps it up quickly by fastening on his usual ending.

What Else Is There to Say?

We've probably all been in a situation where we've worked hard on a paper. All that remains is the conclusion. We read over what we've written and then struggle to think of anything else to add. We've already said everything. After staring at the paper, we decide to revert back to our tried-and-true closing statement: "Now you know everything about . . . [topic]."

It's common for students to get tired of the topic and the paper by the time they've reached the conclusion. It's not easy to sustain one's attention and motivation over an extended period of time. Not infrequently, the lack of intensity of the conclusion reflects this. Students run out of steam. How can we reenergize students at this point so they don't revert back to their old standbys? How can we motivate them to go beyond, "I liked writing this report," and continue to think about the needs of the reader? To go back to what Karen Tracey wrote, "We do research to answer our own questions, and we write up research to answer the questions of others" (1997, p. 10).

How do we encourage writers to think about the questions that still remain in the reader's mind or perhaps to push those questions to a new level?

We believe all students are capable of writing effective conclusions. We also believe that students would be reenergized, even after spending weeks on a project, if they had at their disposal a range of strategies and concrete examples of how others have used them. Then, they could move beyond standard conclusions and experiment with different types of endings. Our experiences suggest that most students revert back to the "usual" endings because they don't know how to bring closure in any other way.

Conclusions, like leads, take time to create. They don't just pop into a writer's head (as a general rule). It's important to work on endings, nevertheless, because they play an important role in the paper. The conclusion helps form the reader's final impression of the report.

Although there are several ways to end a report, some endings will work better than others, depending on the tone of the report, the writer's style, the nature of the research question, the topic selected, and so forth. Before they can decide on a strategy to use, writers need to think about what they want to accomplish through their conclusions. The final words or sentences in a paper may

- connect the beginning and end of the paper, forming an organized whole
- link together multiple, diverse ideas
- recap key point(s)
- provide next steps
- lead readers to future considerations
- draw a final conclusion
- let the reader know what impact the topic has had on the writer
- challenge the reader to continue to think about the topic in a more sophisticated way.

What Is a "Clincher"?

One day, before beginning a series of lessons on conclusions, Mary asked a group of fourth graders to write down what they thought about when they wrote conclusions. She wanted them to explain what they tried to do in the conclusion. Ken wrote, "Have a good clincher." Dominick responded, "Put a clincher with really good words that can knock people's socks off." Janeen suggested, "I think about what I wrote and how I wrote it and I make a clincher out of the facts." The word "clincher" was in almost every response. Mary was sure that the teacher had worked on conclusions with these children. Mary had heard the teacher tell the children that their writing would "knock the socks off the readers," so she was only slightly surprised to see Dominick echo the teacher's words.

These fourth graders clearly knew how important it was to pay attention to their endings. They knew what the conclusion was supposed to do, but did they know how to write effective conclusions? Maybe or maybe not. Embedded in this question is a subtle but important distinction: it's one thing to know why one writes a conclusion (so you can knock the people's socks off) and another to know how to write a conclusion (i.e., to be able to compose effective clinchers—to know what good clinchers sound like and look like). This fourth-grade teacher was on the right track. She recognized that to teach the students to move from an abstract term like "clincher" to its concrete application, she would need to share with them many good examples of effective conclusions. In addition, she would need to talk with them about what the author did to create the conclusion, what purpose the conclusion served, how the author crafted it, how it connected to the rest of the piece, and so on. She would need to model well-written and not-so-well-written attempts at closure and think aloud as she worked her way through the process of analyzing them.

Below you'll find several conclusion strategies that you may share with your students. As with the strategies for leads, we arranged these strategies from easier to more difficult. Included in the introduction to Part 2, you may recall, are the specific procedures we used to teach strategies to our students. You may want to refer back to that section before introducing conclusion strategies in your classes. We employ the same instructional procedures to introduce all the strategies. Some of the strategies listed below are clearly more sophisticated than others. Consider the research question or thesis statement and the developmental level of the student when determining which strategies to teach.

Strategies

1. Dreaming of the Future

The article concludes with the author wondering about future possibilities for his topic.

Example: The author of this article about a military vehicle, the Light Armored Vehicle-25, presents a vision of how the common citizen might use this vehicle in the future. He writes:

> A different model [Light Armored Vehicle-25], now being used by the Marines to haul food and ammunition, could soon be used by nonmilitary drivers, particularly as ambulances. Or perhaps as something a

little more fun, for those who can afford the $900,000 price tag. Maybe something like a monster RV. Think how that would look on your next camping trip.

T. Andrews, "Rough Rider," Boys' Life, March 2000, 17.

Student Example: This strategy awakened Alex's imagination.

I am very happy that I chose submarines as my research project. There are some facts that are so incredible that I could not believe. For instance how fast they can travel and how hot the nuclear reactor can get. I think submarines in the future will be able to open and close while they're underwater, so other submarines can exit the ship. Maybe in the future submarines will be able to have windows.

Teacher to Teacher This strategy works particularly well with topics that concern technology and their future developments. It also works for endangered animal reports or reports on current issues, such as air pollution.

2. Posing a Question

The author asks a thought-provoking question to get the reader to continue to think about the topic after the piece has been read.

Example: The author of this article about active volcanoes ends with

When the fury stops, Montserrat may yet rebuild just as those around Mount St. Helens did. Who will have to rebuild next?

W. Roessing, "Tick, Tick, Tick," Boys' Life, May 2000, 33.

Student Example: Writers want their readers to keep thinking about the topic well after the last word is read. Lynette accomplishes this by posing this question to conclude her report on penguins: "Do you ever wonder what penguins will make their nests out of 1,000 years from now?" We've never thought about this, but it's clear that Lynette's research has raised this question for her. It is an intriguing one, isn't it? She's really dreaming of the future as she poses this question.

Teacher to Teacher Several tips come to mind for this strategy: First, you may need to review the difference between big and little questions before you introduce this strategy (see Chapter 2). Students may need to be reminded that they should think of big, involved questions for the conclusion. Questions such as "Did you learn something new about [the topic]?" or "Would you like to find out more?" are not effective conclusions.

Second, some students may take this opportunity to think of a question that relates to their topic, but goes beyond the scope of their reports. They should be reminded that the purpose of the conclusion isn't to add a new idea at the end of the report; rather, it is to get the reader to ponder more deeply what was presented in the report.

Finally, when working with younger or less experienced writers, you may want to brainstorm some "question words" to get the students started: "What if," "could," "should," "when," "if," "does," "where," "how," and so forth.

3. Ask a Question and Answer It

The author concludes by asking a question and then supplying the answer in the same paragraph.

Example: In this article, the author introduces readers to shrimp that clean other fish in the ocean, picking off dead skin and pieces of food with their tiny claws. The article concludes with a question and an answer:

What's in it for the shrimps? They turn their pickings into a tasty meal!

"Spring Cleaning," *National Geographic for Kids!*, April/May 2002, 24.

Student Example: Sara may not have actually asked a question, but she did ponder an interesting point: "I wonder if Monet will always be considered to be a great artist. I certainly think he will be."

Teacher to Teacher   Please see suggestions under "Posing a Question" above.

4. "Although"

The author ends the paper or report by contrasting a piece of information with the main point of the article. The first word of this conclusion is "Although."

Example: This article provides a snapshot of Mattie Stepanek, an eleven-year-old boy who is the author of two best-selling books of poems. Mattie suffers from a rare form of muscular dystrophy. The article concludes:

Although much of what he writes about is sad, Mattie's message is one of hope . . .

K. Hoffman, "Poems from the Heart," *Time for Kids,* 25 January 2002, 7.

Student Example: Kathryn signals closure to her report with "Although" and then gives the reader one more idea to ponder.

Although the universe may seem like a big blue sky with the sun, earth, and other planets, it is much more complicated that that, as you can see. There are stars, meteors, comets, planets, and of course, the Earth. Here on Earth, scientists continue to research how the universe began. Is the Big Bang theory really true? The only remains of the original fireball from the Big Bang explosion are faint radio waves. Scientists are searching for a theory that merges quantum mechanics and gravity, but haven't found one yet. They hope the string theory will tie together gravity and quantum mechanics to help them explore further back in time to reveal the truth. With all the theories in the world, there are many different answers to how the universe began. This big question, "How did the universe start?" still awaits a final answer.

Teacher to Teacher   Teachers should review what different conjunctions signify and signal so that the contrasting elements stand out.

5. "Finally"

Many writers signal the end of their piece by beginning the last paragraph with the word "finally."

Example: The author of this article about veterinarians begins the last paragraph with

Finally, if your pet is doing well after treatment, let your veterinarian and the staff know. They grow fond of the animals that come into their lives, too. "The best phone calls I get," says Rider, "are the ones that say everything is going great."

S. Sawicki, "Vet Savvy," *Animals,* January/February 2000, 33, 38.

Student Example: Barbara had each of her students create a mandala (a circle with symbols that represent things that are important to them). In addition, she had them write a piece that provided a rationale for the items they included. Sarah concluded her mandala with "Finally, the flag of the United States of America means that I [am] Patriotic for my country."

6. Help!

The author lets the reader know that help is needed.

Example: In this article of the El Salvador earthquake, the author ends with

> El Salvador's President Francisco Flores appealed to other nations to send supplies and help his country rebuild.
>
> R. Upadhyay, "One Crushing Quake," *Time for Kids*, 26 January, 2001, 6.

Student Example: Chloe ends her autobiography in an unusual way. Her love of animals is evident, as the reader can see from her closing plea:

> This year I was very lucky that I adopted a puppy from the pound and gave her a good life. I hope people will help animals and keep them from being endangered.

Teacher to Teacher   This fits exceptionally well with topics that shout out for a call to action. It encourages writers to think about ways in which people can make a difference. Students may encourage others to support organizations, such as the World Wildlife Foundation, that work to rescue endangered animals.

7. No Doubt About It!

The author ends the piece by drawing one indisputable conclusion about his topic. Phrases such as "One thing seems certain," "Without a doubt," or "There is no question" may signal the use of this strategy.

Example: An example of this strategy can be found in an article that describes how medical improvements allow people to live longer. The author concludes with

> One thing seems certain: we have longer healthier lives to look forward to!
>
> R. Upadhyay, "Will We Live to Be 150?" *Time for Kids*, 21 January, 2000, 11–12.

Student Examples: This strategy leaves no room for doubt; the report is coming to an end. Lisa, a seventh grader, found this strategy helpful in concluding her report on the Holocaust.

> There is one thing that is certain. It is that the Holocaust showed millions of people that suffering and death can promote compassion. . . . This event will scar the people of the world forever and it will never be forgotten . . .

Could a fifth grader handle this strategy? You bet. In fact, Sabina goes one further. She brings closure to her report on pandas by combining this strategy and "Posing a Question":

> Whether pandas live in the wild or at a zoo, one thing is certain. Pandas are almost extinct because man has destroyed the places where bamboo grows. Homes and buildings have been constructed where tall bamboo once was. Even in areas where bamboo is still growing it is scarce and takes two or three years to grow back. And within those two or three years, what will happen to the pandas?

Teacher to Teacher Before having students use this strategy, review the differences between facts and opinions. If they're sharing an opinion, you may want it to be grounded in facts from their research.

---

8. Giving Advice

The author ends the piece by providing a bit of advice or a suggestion.

Example: Thomas realizes life is too short to be unhappy. His advice: "Make the most of it, and go right ahead and do your stuff" (T. J. Murphy, "Playing a Brain," *Boys' Life*, March 2000, 12).

Student Examples: Here's the way Bradley, a seventh grader, used this strategy in his report about automobile pollution. Notice how he embeds his advice in the concluding paragraph and goes on to tell why we should heed it:

> Cars cause lots of pollution and there should be something done to stop that. My advice is don't drive if you don't need to and help save the environment by taking buses, trains, etc. Automobiles are very harmful to the environment. It causes smog, acid rain, global warming, and many other harmful things that are dangerous to us, animals, plants and the environment. I think there is something that could be done.

We don't doubt, in this example, that Shawna's advice is based on her research, but we think she's probably heard it from her parents, too. What do you think?

All my sources say that melanoma is an easy type of cancer to battle. But you need to help watch for it and battle it. My advice to you is don't get too much sun and wear sunscreen. If you spend a day on the beach, make sure you can go under an umbrella or someplace you can go to get out of the sun.

Teacher to Teacher Some students may not understand the difference between giving advice and offering an opinion. In order to help make a distinction, it may be necessary to define "advice" clearly. When giving advice, one offers suggestions or recommendations. An opinion, on the other hand, is an expression of one's view or beliefs. Students who are confused may find it helpful to begin with "I'd suggest . . ."

9. Sharing an Emotion

The author describes the emotional effect the topic has had on him.

Example: This article is about a group of young people who spent time cleaning up a neighborhood. The author lets the reader know how they are feeling as the day winds down.

It may sound weird, but at the end of such a hard and dirty day, the cleanup crew all felt good. They knew they'd made a place they love just a little bit better.

F. Asch, "Cleanup at Otter Creek," *Ranger Rick,* 34, no. 4, April 2000, 16.

Student Example: A writer's voice often comes alive when she can express her feeling about her topic. This strategy grants students permission to let the reader know that there is a person behind the pen. Catherine started her research assuming (incorrectly) that the number of white-tailed deer were declining. Little did she suspect that this was not true. Her voice shines through with her honest concluding statement.

Despite the fact that this kind of deer is hunted for their buckskin because of their tremendous warmth, you're a little surprised to read that the population of the white-tailed deer has been increasing over the years rather than decreasing. Well, I was surprised!

We suggest that colleagues go over some emotion words before introducing this strategy: "impressed," "astonished," "disappointed," "intimidated," "awestruck," "captivated," "fascinated," "mesmerized," and "worried." This is a great way to build vocabulary. Students who write common words such as "glad" or "surprised" may be encouraged to look in a thesaurus or dictionary to find a more descriptive word.

10. What's Next?

The author concludes by telling the reader what the final step in a sequence of events will be.

Example: In an article about Casey Martin, a disabled golfer who wants to use a golf cart in a tournament, the author notes that the U.S. Supreme Court is now hearing the case. The article ends with, "The court is expected to rule by July." ("The Case of Casey's Cart," *Time for Kids*, 26 January 2001, 2).

This short statement lets the reader know what's expected to happen next. There is no need to write anything else. The reader knows he's at the end of the article.

Student Example: We know what the next steps are for Willy, an ambitious fifth grader, by the conclusion he crafted for his autobiography:

> For the possibility for me to complete my dreams, I would take lots of time and effort to be a mathematician. When I am in high school, I will have to search and find very good colleges with strong math classes and I would have to be well rounded. Then in college I will need to get an advanced degree. In order to play pro basketball, I would need to practice a lot. I would also need to keep my grades up, so that I will be able to play college basketball first. To be drafted would be the hard part. But maybe I will be able to do it!

Did you notice that Willy's conclusion sounds like Dreaming of the Future? Looking closer, however, we see he's added another dimension. He acknowledges what needs to be done in order for this dream to become a reality. He's told us what's next in his list of things to do.

This strategy is usually most effective when the conclusion is short, to the point, and clearly the last step in the logical progression of ideas.

11. Right Now

The author concludes by bringing the reader up-to-date. He describes the topic's current condition, often using the word "today" to signal this strategy.

Example: The author of this fascinating article about chocolate uses this strategy to bring the reader from about A.D. 600 to the present. She concludes with

> Today, scientists and chocolate makers are working to make chocolate products that are lower in fat and sugar. If they succeed, you might have to think twice about calling candy bars junk food.
>
> A. Conover, "Pass the Chocolate," *National Geographic for Kids!* October 2000, 13–15.

Student Example: Todd worked on a research paper in which he questioned whether or not humans should be cloned. He cited all kinds of facts, including a 1997 poll that asked people if they thought it was "unethical and against God's will to clone humans." He concludes his paper by compellingly bringing to bear what we need to consider right now:

> We are on the verge of achieving the ability to clone humans. With more research it will be possible. If the ability is obtained it will release a myriad of questions about ethics and who should have access to the technology. The research should not continue. In conclusion, please postpone the clone.

Teacher to Teacher

To apply this strategy, students need to use current resources. You may need to help students find them if they aren't familiar with this type of research. Encourage students to combine this strategy with Dreaming of the Future. For example, students might trace the evolution of racism or terrorism to see how it has developed to its present state and conclude by hypothesizing what its future might be.

12. "No Matter" Plus Draw a Conclusion

The author begins with the words "No matter." Next he draws a conclusion.

Example: The author of this article about Olympic figure skaters combines "No Matter" Plus Draw a Conclusion with No Doubt About It! to produce a very effective conclusion

No matter who wins, one thing is certain: The world can expect a night of dazzling skating.

N. G. Cutler, "Queens of the Ice," Time for Kids, February 2002, 7.

Student Examples: We decided to see if fourth graders who were working on book reports could use this strategy to signal closure. Larry and Susan found that it worked well for their reports. Larry reviewed a book about Missouri. In the report, he notes Missouri's "unpredictable climate" and goes on to explain that several records had been set. He concluded his report with "No matter how bad the weather can get, I would like to live there."

Susan's book report was about beagles. Near the end of the report she explains how some beagles are trained to sniff out dangerous items and to find termites. She concludes with "No matter how many jobs the beagle has, it probably still has time to play."

Teacher to Teacher This strategy may seem simple, but to use it effectively, writers must synthesize the key points of the report and then draw a conclusion based on the evidence they found in their research. Because there is so much critical thinking involved in this strategy, it is challenging, but with modeling, students can be very successful.

---

13. Providing a Summary

The author recaps the key points in the article or report in the last paragraph.

Examples: This article gives a brief history of the American flag and what Old Glory symbolizes. The author pulls the entire article together by summarizing the key points in the two closing paragraphs:

> Old Glory has changed in many small ways since 1777. Yet its bold design remains unmistakable. Francis Hopkinson, in fact, would almost certainly recognize today's flag.
>
> And he'd be proud to see that Americans still love the broad stripes, the bright stars, and the republic for which they stand.

P. Winkler, "Broad Stripes and Bright Stars," National Geographic for Kids!
April/May 2002, 19–22.

It's not difficult to recognize the key points in this article about volcanoes. The author concludes

As you can see, volcanoes are not all bad. They might be scary to watch and frightening to hear, but the paths of destruction they carve are often followed by new life and abundant growth.

K. Uretsky, "When the Earth Explodes," Cricket, September 1999, 47–50.

Student Example: It's not easy to whittle down an entire report into a sentence or two, but Chloe came back to the one idea she hoped to convey in her report on Japan:

As you can see there are many interesting things about Japan. There are a lot of differences and some similarities in growing up in Japan and in the U.S.

Teacher to Teacher   Many students often begin with "As you can see," which gives them a framework for summarizing what they have written. Remind students to keep their summaries short and to avoid repeating what they have already written.

---

14. Connecting Beginning and End

The author connects information from the first paragraph to information in the final paragraph. Often the same words are repeated in both parts of the report or article.

Examples: The opening paragraph of an article about wild ponies begins with, "Cheers rise as the ponies splash into the water." The article goes on to explain that each July local cowboys from Assateague, an island off the coast of Virginia and Maryland, round up wild ponies and herd them across a narrow channel to Chincoteague, a nearby island, where thousands of spectators come to watch as the ponies are auctioned off.

The article ends with this paragraph:

The day after the auction, Chincoteague cowboys herd the ponies back to the water's edge. Crowds cheer again as the ponies swim home to Assateague Island. There they will be free to roam again for another year. [Notice how the author begins with the ponies leaving home and ends with the ponies returning home. In the first sentence of the article and in the last paragraph, the author uses the word "cheer(s)."]

"Wild Ponies: Assateague Island's Mane Attraction," National Geographic for Kids!
April/May 2002, 4–8.

In this story about the 2000 Summer Olympics, the author begins with a statement about the Olympic flame:

It has traveled nearly 17,000 miles, burning brightly on land and sea, in the air and even underwater. Through 1,000 towns in 100 days, the Olympic flame has been winding . . .

In the rest of the article, the author compares and contrasts the games of 2,800 years ago with those of today. She questions who will win the medals and concludes by coming back to the idea of the flame:

We'll know the answer by the time the Olympic flame is snuffed out on October 1. Until then, we can cheer on our favorites and bask in the happy glow from the other side of the world.

M. Pickerill, "Faster, Higher, Stronger," *Time for Kids,* 15 September 2000, 4–6.

Student Examples: Although this is a common strategy for teachers to share with students, it's often easier said than done. It would seem that the writer would merely start at point A and return to point A at the end. We've found, however, that many students move so far away from their original idea that by the time they get to the end, they could never find their way back. This strategy reminds us of balancing a checkbook—if all the checks throughout the month are not carefully accounted for, the checkbook will not balance at the end of the month. Likewise, if all the pieces of the report are not tightly connected, the writer cannot logically start with point A and return to it at the end.

Erin, a fifth grader, deserves a great deal of credit. She begins and ends her report on dragons with her use of "snow." Notice how cleverly she loops back to her beginning. Her lead paragraph read:

You've gone back 2.1 million years to the time of dragons or so to speak. There are no humans or animals, except for the dragons. You see flaming blasts of fire and ice gulches at the same time. It's snowing but the temperature is 64 degrees F. You see a great sumac tree vanish into thin air. You're walking down the dirt path and see a dragon. You wonder how will this dragon react to your being there? Are you scared or are you excited? What are its powers? What kind is it? Is it friendly? Do you wonder if you're ever going to get home?

She presents a great deal of interesting information about dragons throughout her report and ends with

You have just been teleported back from the time of dragons to the hot muggy summer. With all your knowledge you wonder whom to tell? Will anyone believe you? You decide not to tell anyone. Then you ask yourself "What if one came home with you?" You looked out the window. It started snowing! That answered your question once and for all.

How about this for a tidy little conclusion? Ken, a fourth grader, reported on a book he read about New Hampshire. His lead explained that New Hampshire is in the northeastern part of the United States and that "it is known for its lakes, famous people and the products it makes." He concluded the report by combining two strategies: "No Matter" Plus Draw a Conclusion and Connecting Beginning and End. He writes, "No matter if you go to see the lakes, famous people or the products it makes, it will always be exciting."

Teacher to Teacher   See Appendix A for examples of picture books that employ this strategy.

---

15. Quote

The author finds an appropriate quote from her research that can bring closure to the piece.

Examples: This article describes how two middle school students from Maryland are trying to increase the number of oysters in the Chesapeake Bay. The oysters help the environment by using their bodies to purify the water. The article concludes with a quote from one of the girls involved in this project: "Jamie adds, 'We have to help because we live here too'" (E. Murphy, "Bringing Up Baby Oysters," *National Geographic for Kids!* October 2001, 23).

In this article about a British archaeologist who found ancient gold coins in London, the author concludes with the archaeologist's words:

But Severn never imagined he would dig up such a treasure himself. "This is the find of a lifetime," he says.

M. Pickerill, "Buried Treasure," *Time for Kids*, 26 January 2001, 7.

Student Example: Locating just the right quote is key to the success of this strategy. It has to signal "the end." Greg, a fifth grader, hunted for the perfect quote to concluded his report on Picasso and found it.

Picasso never knew what would happen when he picked up a paintbrush. He said art was like a bird's song. Why try to understand it? On April 8, 1973, Pablo Picasso died at Mougins, France, at the age of 91. He was painting at dawn on the final day of his long, long life. He left behind all his possessions, his wives, his children, and 78 years of artwork. He made so much artwork that it's hard to believe it all came from one lifetime. He once said, "Creation is the only thing that interests me."

☑ Checking In with Nick

We've been following Nick throughout the researching and reporting process. He's spent quite a bit of time revising his report to make it much more detailed and focused than his original. Now he's ready to work on his conclusion. Here's what he's written so far.

Certain to Survive?

It's newborn body weighs only 2 oz., but eventually it will eat about 30 pounds of food each day. Who could eat this much food? An African elephant? A Great White Shark? Nope. The one with the big appetite is the cuddly panda.

You may be wondering where they get all this food. Actually, they eat mostly bamboo, which can be found only in southwest China. It's sad to say that only about 1,000 of them live in the wild and another 100 live in zoos around the world. Why are there so few and what are people doing to protect them?

A long time ago, hunters killed pandas for their fur. It was used for rugs. The pandas had thick fur that kept them warm in their cold weather.

When Pandas were first discovered, they were killed so scientists could study their skin and bones. They were trying to learn more about them. They knew they looked sort of like bears but they didn't hibernate like bears and they can't walk on their hind legs. Also, pandas can grab onto bamboo easily because one of their bones in their wrists is larger and longer than the others. They also have strong jaws and strong teeth witch helps them eat the hard bamboo. If you was a scientist wouldn't you want to find out about all these unique things about pandas too?

Another reason there are so few pandas is because people have built homes and farms in the mountain valleys of China where pandas used to live. The pandas had to move up into the colder mountains to get food and water. This was not good because they ran out of their food supply and because they had to live closer to men who could kill them.

Today the Chinese government is protecting pandas and their land. It's now against the law to kill them and officials plant bamboo so pandas always have enough food.

Although man has killed lots of pandas in the past now people everywhere want to help pandas. Pandas have been brought to zoos where zookeepers give them vitamins and put them on special diets to keep them healthy. Sometimes they live in dark, air-conditioned sections of the zoo, so they feel like they are at home in the mountains of China. Pandas like to be near water, so zookeepers make sure they have plenty to use for drinking, playing and cooling off. Pandas who live in the wild usually live about 15 years. Pandas who live in captivity can live into their 20s.

Today Nick is attempting to revise his original conclusion: "I hope you liked my report. If you want to find out more about panda bears you can go to the library." He drafted several possible conclusions before deciding on the one to use. First he tried No Doubt About It! for his report. What do you think?

There is no question in my mind that the number of panda bears in the world can increase only if everyone works hard to allow them to live their lives the way they did before they were discovered by man.

Nick liked this conclusion but wasn't sure it captured what he was really trying to say. He was fascinated by the fact that pandas eat 30 pounds of food a day. He used this fact with the lead and looped back to it by trying Connecting Beginning and End. Here's what this attempt became:

If the pandas can continue to eat 30 pounds of food each day in a safe environment, they certainly will be able to survive. If not, their future may not be too bright. Only time will tell.

After rereading his entire report with this ending, Nick was concerned that although he connected the beginning and end, his concluding statement was an oversimplification of the problem. He kept working on the report's ending and when all was said and done, Nick decided to combine "No Matter" Plus Draw a Conclusion with Dreaming of the Future to end his piece.

No matter if the pandas live in China or in a zoo, it seems that everyone is now working hard to make sure they live long, safe lives. Perhaps this will help keep pandas from becoming extinct so people in years to come can also enjoy these cuddly-looking animals.

Nick knew that this ending was a much better "clincher" than his original. It draws the reader back to his key point and then leaves him with a final idea to think about—something his original ending did not do.

Stage 9: Presentation

Many teachers like to provide students with opportunities to demonstrate what they've learned by having them prepare a presentation. As you may recall, Barbara mentions this in a letter she sends home to parents (see Figure 3.7). She explains the presentation to parents by writing,

> I also want students to prepare visual presentations to go along with their reports. They may be models, dioramas, three-dimensional representations, or any other appropriate examples that illustrate one aspect of the research paper. *I do not want students to begin this undertaking until the second draft is completed on December 7* although they should be thinking about ideas for this earlier. Presentations will be made on Tuesday, December 18, through Thursday, December 20.

The Massachusetts English Language Arts Curriculum Framework now includes a standard for oral presentations. Standard 3 reads, "Students will make oral presentations that demonstrate appropriate consideration of audience, purpose, and the information to be conveyed" (p. 7). We imagine many states have similar expectations.

In Barbara's room, students begin working on their visual presentations when the second drafts of their reports are finished. Although this is a fairly open-ended assignment, Barbara expects them to follow some basic guidelines. For example, they may use note cards, but they cannot read the report (or pieces of it). Also, they are encouraged to include original art work (either done by hand or created with drawing tools on the computer). Barbara discourages students from photocopying pictures and information from sources and pasting them on a poster. Rather, she asks students to construct or find interesting objects they can share, making the presentation more hands-on. Some students may make PowerPoint presentations to emphasize the highlights of what they have learned. The students love this.

Throughout the book, we've shared pieces of work by several of Barbara's fifth graders. Their written work was of the highest caliber, and their visual presentations were outstanding. Let's follow up on four of them: Steve, Chloe, Greg, and Elizabeth. You may recall that Steve's report focused on whether or not UFOs are real. To enhance his presentation, he crafted a flying saucer set amid flashing disco lights. His peers were fascinated with the information he presented and the clever visual.

Chloe, who wrote about life in Japan, prepared her visual with a little help from her dad, something Barbara approves of. Together they built a Japanese house out of small pieces of wood. Chloe presented it as she explained what she learned about Japanese homes and the traditions of the Japanese.

Greg, who was interested in the diverse periods of Picasso's life and work, created a diorama of *Guernica*. The replication of this masterpiece was astonishing. But that was only the beginning. It turned out that Greg's grandfather was an artist, too. For the second part of his presentation he showed a selection of his grandfather's artwork in a book. Beside each picture of his grandfather's, Greg created the same picture. He was painstakingly bringing his grandfather's works to life again through these reproductions.

Finally, you may recall that Elizabeth was comparing and contrasting figure skating and recreational skating. She created a video for her presentation. This was not your average video, however. It took place in several venues. At first, Elizabeth was at her home, talking to her audience about skating. She then set the context for her audience, explaining what they'd see in the next portion of the video. She moved to the rink and interviewed her skating instructor. On the video, she also demonstrated various skating maneuvers. Her passion for her topic and the content knowledge she gleaned is evident throughout. Oral presentations take the research process to a different level. They personalize the research.

Barbara's class spends portions of three days, usually before a vacation if possible, sharing their projects. By spreading these presentations over three days, Barbara keeps the students highly interested and attentive. It's always an exciting time for the fifth graders and the adults who have supported them through this process.

Regrettably, it's outside the scope of this book to elaborate on oral presentations. Fortunately, however, there are many wonderful resources that can be used to get information about oral presentations. These include *Write Source 2000* (see "Preparing a Speech") (Sebranek, Meyer, and Kemper 1995) and *Teaching Oral Communication in Grades K–8* (Chaney and Burk 1998). You'll also find an excellent rubric for assessing presentations at www.ncsu.edu/midlink/rub.pres.html.

What's Next?

It's time to think about assessment. Nick has come a long way, we believe, but how can we mark this growth in an objective way? How can we let parents, other teachers, administrators, and perhaps people from the state department of education know that Nick and his classmates are able to apply skills and strategies to produce high-quality writing? Before we can answer this question, we may need to ask, "What is 'high-quality writing'?" In the final chapter, we will address these questions. We'll consider our own classroom-based assessment tools as well as rubrics and assessment practices used in states around the country to assess writing performance.

CHAPTER SEVEN

Did We Succeed? Assessment

*You can weigh the calf as much as you want, but it won't grow
unless you feed it.*
—L. Mabry, *Writing to the Rubric*

We believe that it's important for students to be able to evaluate their own development as writers. Before they can do this, however, they need to know what makes "good" informational writing. Students are able to judge the quality of writing only after they have had many opportunities to hear and think about a wide range of expository texts. Results from a recent study by Dell (2000) indicate, nevertheless, that young children may be exposed to very little informational writing in the early grades.

Dell conducted a study of twenty first-grade classrooms (ten from low socioeconomic schools and ten from high socioeconomic schools). She sought to determine the ratio of informational versus narrative texts in these classrooms. She focused her study on three sets of data: the amount of print displayed in the classrooms, the types of books and magazines in the classroom libraries, and the amount of time devoted to informational reading and writing. She coded over 6,000 pieces of print on the walls and surfaces of the classroom. She found that on average 2.6 percent of the 6,023 pieces of print displayed in the classrooms was informational. She classified over 12,000 books and magazines from the classroom libraries during four visits. Only 9.8 percent of the texts in the classroom libraries on her first visit was informational. Finally, she observed the amount of time children spent in written activities (i.e., informational reading and writing). Amazingly, these twenty first-grade classrooms spent on average 3.6 minutes per day reading and writing information texts. Clearly, this study illustrates the scarcity of informational texts available in first grades, regardless of the location of the classrooms. One wonders whether these results are indicative of the experiences of most primary grade students. If this is the case, it may be that many students enter third grade with little experience with expository texts.

It's understandable that students need to recognize the craft of writing before they can seriously critique the quality of their own work or the work of their peers. Graves (1992) noted that students usually know when their writing is good, but they cannot verbalize why it is good. Graves suspects this is because they don't know what elements make up good writing (p. 90). Many students understand that a good piece of expository writing should reflect the writer's content knowledge, exhibit strong writing skills, and reflect the writer's passion for her topic. But how can we make these abstract ideas applicable for a student in the upper elementary or middle school?

Students may be introduced to informational writing in many ways. Perhaps one of the most effective ways to convey what good expository writing looks and sounds like is by exploring well-written informational texts (magazines, biographies, memoirs, informational poems, and so on) across the curriculum. Barbara spends time, especially at the beginning of the year, reading aloud quality informational texts to her fifth graders. Many of these books are picture books. They go slowly, discussing points along the way, making connections, building content knowledge, and noting the author's craft. In the past, upper elementary and middle school teachers have typically shied away from using picture books with their students, thinking that they would be too babyish. Barbara fell into this category. Recent trends in publishing, however, have changed all that. Today there are hundreds of picture books that are designed for older students. The content and language is geared to the preteen and early teenage audience. Appendix A contains a list of picture books that could be used to illustrate specific elements of writing or to demonstrate more generally how accomplished authors employ expository writing to share new ideas and concepts in engaging ways. Allocating time to share these types of books with upper elementary and middle school students is a necessary prerequisite for expository writing instruction. For us, it was definitely time well spent.

Responding to Drafts

By mid-October, Barbara had devoted several weeks to teaching her students about researching and report writing. Along the way, she relied on perhaps the most authentic form of ongoing assessment available to teachers: kidwatching. Through kidwatching, or focused observations, Barbara was able to determine the needs of each student and the impact of her teaching. She observed how the class went through the processes of determining a research question and then collecting and organizing data. She listened to their conversations and the feedback they received from and gave to their classmates. The information she gathered informed her instruction.

Now it was time to look closely at the products they were producing and determine how well they were applying what they had been taught. On November 13, Barbara's students submitted the first drafts of their research reports. Although we call these "first" drafts, they are much more than an initial sketch of ideas. Students are expected to include evidence of the skills and strategies they have been learning about and practicing in class. After carefully reading the drafts, Barbara provides each student with a typed sheet of comments. She prints one copy of the comments for the students to refer to while revising their papers and keeps one copy for herself. She looks at this copy when assessing the final draft. Barbara tells the students that their final grade will be based on how much their writing has improved from draft to final copy. She also explains to them that when she grades their final papers, she looks back at the copies of the first drafts. To determine this growth, she rereads the comments she gave them on their first draft and looks to see what revisions were made with regard to her comments.

In addition to the comment sheet, Barbara structures part of a day so she can confer with students individually. Students are able to work independently on activities so that Barbara can give her undivided attention to the student with whom she is conferring. If possible, Barbara asks Title I, ESL, or assistant teachers to sit in during these times so that they also understand student expectations. She goes over each sheet and explains what needs to be done. From November 13 through December 7, students work on making the meaning clearer, having the papers better organized, adding voice to what they've written, and using strategies to improve leads, transitions, and conclusions. Three weeks may seem like a long time for revision, but during this same time, there are early release days for parent conferences, Thanksgiving break, and time devoted to additional instruction on the research projects. Second drafts (i.e., evidence of revisions of content) are due on December 7. From December 7 until December 14, when the final paper is due, students work on conventions (spelling, sentence structure, punctuation, capitalization, grammar).

Student Accountability

We feel strongly that if teachers take time to make specific comments, students need to understand their responsibility to follow through with implementing suggestions. Barbara works closely with the children and follows through on the feedback she gives. The underlying purpose for the assessment is to provide each student with an honest response, which includes concrete, specific suggestions for ways to grow. Barbara makes sure that all support faculty (Title I, ESL, reading specialists, special needs teachers, and so on) have copies of the comments so they can provide additional support to the students who need it.

Let's look at the feedback that three fifth graders received from Barbara on their research reports.

Betty

Betty, a struggling writer, received Barbara's typed comments on her first draft about the cobra. Barbara encouraged Betty to work on three specific areas that had been introduced throughout this research project: (1) identify her research question (thesis); (2) adjust her voice/word choice, and (3) include effective transitions:

> Betty,
>
> You certainly did find out lots of information about the cobra. This snake is truly a fascinating animal!
>
> Please include your research question. What animal are you comparing and contrasting with the cobra? Is it another type of snake?
>
> Here are some general suggestions for your paper.
>
> Leave out
> "Now I will tell you . . ."
> "Now you know . . ."
> "Now here's where they live."
> "Here's something cool."
> "So that wraps up . . ."
>
> Include transitions by connecting your ideas. For example, see how you can relate the fangs of the cobra to the topic about enemies. Try "Repeat a Word." For example, you may say something like "Because their fangs are so poisonous, the enemies of the cobra must be able to surprise it. That's why birds are so effective. They can surprise the cobra by swooping down and . . ."
>
> I will help you with the transitions. First, include your research question. Then write the topic you are discussing in the margins. We'll work on transitions then and do the conclusion later.
>
> Sincerely,
> Mrs. Siegel
>
> _____
> Parent Signature

Looking at the first drafts, providing specific, concrete suggestions and then comparing first and final papers enables Barbara to determine how well the students are applying the skills and strategies she has been reinforcing through her instruction. Below is a copy of the letter Barbara wrote to Betty after receiving her final paper. Notice that she emphasized the same three areas on which she wanted Betty to focus during revision.

> Dear Betty,
>
> I was really pleased to see that you followed through on some of my comments to you on your draft. In particular, you left out the language such as "Now I will tell you . . ." or "Now you know . . ." I can also see where you tried to make connections among some of your ideas by including more transitions. Don't forget that you need to show a relationship among all your topics so that you don't jump from one to another. Thanks for putting in a conclusion, but if you are going to talk about the cobra being endangered, you should give some evidence of it in your paper for the reader to think about.
>
> You forgot to include one of the most important purposes of this research paper: the research question. Remember how I asked you to make sure that you stated it in your first paragraph? Why are you writing this report?
>
> I can see that your paper is improved. Keep on working hard and your next one will be even better.
>
> Sincerely,
> Mrs. Siegel
>
> --
> I have seen the comments regarding my child's final research report.
> Grade = _____
>
> _____
> Parent Signature

Linking Assessment and Instruction

The following excerpts from Elizabeth's and Steve's letters reveal the kind of feedback Barbara gives to various levels of writers. Elizabeth often struggled with organizing ideas when she wrote. However, she knew a great deal about figure skating; she took lessons every Saturday. Her passion for the topic and the use of a compare-and-contrast data chart helped to keep her organized. But even with a structured data chart, which was broken into two major categories (recreational and figure skating), Elizabeth's first draft, although very informative, needed transitions to make it more coherent and less boring. Steve, on the other hand, was the type of student who spent a great deal of time planning what he would say and how he would say it. He carefully organized his paper in his head before he put pencil to paper. As a result, his paper needed very little revision. In each case,

Barbara tried to determine where each writer was developmentally and how she could move the student to the appropriate next level. As you read these excerpts, notice how tightly assessment and instruction are woven together.

Elizabeth

Elizabeth researched the difference between figure skating and recreational skating. She began with this lead: "What is faster than a runner and more elegant than a fashion model?" Elizabeth introduced her topic in a captivating way, but her paper as a whole lacked effective transitions, which Barbara wanted her to focus on in her revision. Barbara made the following comment in her response to this first draft. In this excerpt from Barbara's letter, notice how she gave Elizabeth feedback and provided her with a strategy to organize her ideas into larger pieces.

> In the margin, write what you're contrasting and comparing. For example, some of the topics you cover are moves, competitions, etc. From there, we'll look at ways to connect paragraphs and these topics by using transitions. We'll also find other ways of saying: "Another similarity or another difference."

Barbara wanted Elizabeth to make bigger connections among her ideas and go beyond making lists. She asked Elizabeth to look at page 2 of her report and

> Rewrite and combine the moves. For example, you might say something like, "In both types of skating, there are some basic moves that are very much alike. They are stroke, crossover, and backward skating." Then go on to describe each of these moves in the next few paragraphs.

In other words, Barbara wanted Elizabeth to transition using the Several to One strategy. Elizabeth received specific suggestions for improving her paper and also feedback on what was effective: "Keep your ending. It fits so well here."

In response to Elizabeth's final paper, Barbara wrote:

> Dear Elizabeth,
>   You are so amazing. You followed through on every single suggestion or comment I made to you from your first draft. You have improved your paper so much. It is now clearer to the reader! You managed to discuss so many aspects of figure skating and regular skating without turning it into one long list. You took two very complex sports and compared

and contrasted them in such detail. Your transitions made your ideas flow smoothly so that one topic leads into another.

Elizabeth, I was very impressed with your first draft and this final paper is just so remarkable. You should be so proud of how hard you worked!! I also appreciate all the attention you paid to proofreading what you wrote.

It would have been easier to write: "Add transitions," throughout Elizabeth's paper, but we all know that without specific examples of exactly what "add transitions" means, this feedback is of little use to a writer. Barbara didn't rewrite Elizabeth's paper, but she provided concrete suggestions, referred her to strategies that were introduced in class, and provided additional instruction through this assessment.

Steve

Not all first drafts require extensive revision. Some writers spend a great deal of time thinking about the whole piece before they begin to write. As a result, the first version is often well organized and detailed. Steve is such a writer. He chose to research UFOs. His attention to audience was evident from the start of his paper, which contained an imaginary news report from the National UFO Reporting Center. In this news report Steve specified the dates, times, places, and details of three UFO sightings. This believable news report grabbed the reader's attention immediately. The rest of the draft was equally well done. Barbara noted in her response to his first draft:

Your report is incredibly impressive! What an excellent research job you have done on it. I love your introduction and opening. What a great way to hook the reader! Throughout your paper, your sentences flow into one another. You used transitions well. You spent much time connecting your ideas. I have very little to say to improve your paper. I would encourage you to work with me so [you] could use more sophisticated vocabulary.

Steve heeded Barbara's advice. In response to his final draft, Barbara wrote:

Your draft was absolutely outstanding! I am thrilled that you took the initiative and improved your paper by "fine-tuning" some of your vocabulary.

Barbara then goes on to cite some specific changes Steve made to his paper. One lesson we've learned over the years is to admit that a paper is good if it is and to acknowledge that not all drafts need extensive revisions.

What Purpose Does Feedback Serve?

Giving narrative feedback on student work is one way in which teachers can measure student growth as writers and provide concrete evidence to show this growth. The personal nature of responses to written tasks or to observations is definitely valuable, if well done. The teacher can easily address a boundless array of elements in a response—from the use of metaphors to the proper citation of reference materials. Analyzing student work and kid-watching have proven to be two highly effective means for us to gather data about the quality of student work.

We realize, however, that not all teachers can spend this much time providing students with individual feedback and instruction. Middle school teachers, for example, may have 125 students (or more) in their Language Arts/English classes. To go through this same process with a large number of students all at once would be daunting. There may be other ways to achieve the same objectives, nevertheless. Teachers may think about staggering research reports. Perhaps not every class needs to be doing research projects during the same marking term. It may be possible for different classes to be working on research projects at different points throughout the year, so not all 125 student reports are due at the same time.

In order to cut down on the amount of writing involved in providing feedback, teachers may decide to create a checklist of traits for students to focus on. Figure 7.1 shows how the Focused Feedback Sheet we created may be used to provide feedback. Students could also use this sheet when they engage in peer conferences. This sheet would give students a structured framework within which to provide each other with concrete, constructive feedback. There's space to indicate changes that students should consider and room to include which strategies they might try. As you can see, this sheet can be returned to the student with his first draft and collected again with the final draft. The teacher can easily see whether or not the student focused on the identified areas while revising the paper.

We can't stress enough how important it is to elicit the help of support personnel (special needs teachers, ESL teachers, Title I teachers, student teachers, para-educators, and others) as you work through this process.

Specific feedback throughout the writing process validates what the students are doing. They work hard and need to know that. The feedback on the draft serves as a catalyst for the next stage: revision. Both of us can recall getting papers back with vague comments written on them, such as, "not well organized," or "needs work," or "weak ending." The unfortunate part was that these comments didn't mean anything to us. We didn't know what the teacher meant because the comments were too vague, and we didn't know how to make a "weak ending" any better. Revision often meant changing words around. Conversely, knowing exactly what needs to be done to improve a paper and knowing how to accomplish this is highly

Figure 7.1 Focused Feedback Sheet

Trait	Draft		Final Paper
	Okay	Needs Work—Try:	Comments
Identification of research question or thesis	✓		
Transitions		2nd to 3rd paragraph: Repeat a Word 4th to 5th paragraph: Contrast	
Leads		Right to the Point or What's Wrong?	
Conclusions	✓		
Development of Ideas (Research)		You need to find more information that you can use to contrast with figure skating. Try this web site:	
Organization of Ideas		Add the transition between paragraphs 4 and 5 and to signal the contrast and you'll be fine.	
Word Choice		Count how many times you used the word "skaters." Try other words: "girls, "people who love to skate," etc.	
Mechanics		We'll look at mechanics once the research question is answered completely and clearly.	

motivating for most students. The goal is to teach students how to problem solve so that when they are in a similar situation in the future, they can resolve the problem independently.

Teacher to Teacher   This year, for the first time, parent conferences were scheduled between the time the students submitted their first and second drafts. Having an opportunity to show parents their child's work and discuss this process with them seemed to make a significant difference in their willingness to monitor their child's progress. During these conversations, Barbara explained how hard the children were working and what the next steps in the process would be. She also made sure parents knew that after-school help was available for students who would need or want it. Phone calls were made to parents who could not make it to school for a conference. They received this same information.

Developing Tangible Self-Assessment Tools

Although the teacher plays a key role in the assessment process, sharing this responsibility with students in grades 3 through 8 can produce positive results. Getting students involved in their own assessment pushes them to think metacognitively about the processes and strategies they are using. They need to evaluate what works, what doesn't, and why.

Six-Point Scale for Animal Research

During our first attempt at researching and reporting, we decided to have the students help us design an evaluation scale. We intentionally waited until the students were almost done with the project before we presented the idea of the scale. We knew that we had introduced many new skills and concepts (structuring a report around a big question; using data charts; new strategies of leads, transitions, and conclusions) in a relatively short period of time and believed they would not be ready to design a scale until they had gone through the entire process. They needed to see the whole picture first and then take it apart.

In a large-group setting and with very little guidance from us, the fifth graders were able to create the Six-Point Scale for Animal Research found in Figure 7.2. We began this process by talking about leads. We asked the class to define the characteristics of weak leads and then strong leads. We worked our way down the list of elements, recording the student responses on a white erase board. Little did we know, however, that the process of creating this tool would provide us with an authentic opportunity to review all the thinking we had done throughout the several weeks of this project. The students had to think back to what we discussed along the way. In a sense, it helped us assess what they had learned about researching and report writing and what they had retained from prior lessons.

After typing up the scale, we distributed it in class. Next, we modeled how to use it in assessing our own reports. Using the think-aloud procedure, Mary assessed her raccoon report, emphasizing that the number she circled was not as important as the rationale she had for determining this number. Once the students became comfortable with this procedure, we asked them to assess the rest of Mary's report. She thought it was pretty good, but they were eager to share constructive feedback. We were impressed with the very insightful rationales they attached to their decisions. On a subsequent day, we asked students

Figure 7.2 Six-Point Scale for Animal Research

	Weak		**Strong**
Lead (beginning paragraph)	Tells readers what they will read about;* dull; research question not clearly presented	1 2 3 4 5 6	Lets readers figure out what they will read about, interesting, clear question
Paragraphs	Sentences do not relate to one idea (topic)	1 2 3 4 5 6	Sentences relate to one idea (topic)
Bridge sentence	Tells reader (e.g., "Now I will tell you about . . ."); choppy	1 2 3 4 5 6	Smooth; connects ideas; flows
Ending	Stops short; takes reader nowhere	1 2 3 4 5 6	Brings the whole piece together; connects beginning and end
Organization	Jumps from one idea to the next	1 2 3 4 5 6	Has paragraphs that are sequenced logically; has paragraphs that have complete sentences about one topic
Content	Not enough detail to answer the research question; goes off the topic and answers a different question	1 2 3 4 5 6	Includes enough detail to thoroughly answer the research question; stays on the topic
Voice	Sounds like an encyclopedia	1 2 3 4 5 6	Blends facts and feelings using your own natural language
Spelling	Many misspelled words	1 2 3 4 5 6	No misspelled words
Word Choice	Uses common, nonspecific words	1 2 3 4 5 6	Uses colorful, specific, clear words
Grammar	Errors in use of 's and run-on sentences	1 2 3 4 5 6	Correct use of 's and complete sentences
Punctuation	Many mistakes with punctuation	1 2 3 4 5 6	No mistakes with punctuation

*Many first drafts began, "I am going to tell you about . . . (topic)." Others gave away the entire report in the lead. They would identify their thesis question and answer it in the first paragraph.

Reprinted with permission: Siegel, B., and M. McMackin, 2000. "Research: Merging Inquiry and Writing." Currents in Literacy 3 (1) , Cambridge, MA: Lesley College, 6.

to assess their own reports independently. Some of them were more critical of their work than we might have been. We sat down with these students and pointed out where we saw strengths that they might have overlooked.

Our primary goal in having students create this tool with us was to involve them in the assessment process—to send a message that they need to be the primary evaluators of their own work, that they need to know what makes "good" writing and be able to recognize their own "good" or "not-so-good" writing.

Researching and Reporting Checklist

Although we knew from the onset that researching is a complex process, we weren't aware of exactly how many skills were needed to complete this process successfully. It was at this time that we decided to outline the criteria for writing reports. We wanted to have a simple checklist (Figure 7.3) for the students to follow so they wouldn't get bogged down in the processes of researching and reporting. This checklist highlighted what we wanted the students to focus on as they worked on their reports. It reflected the skills we emphasized in our teaching. Each part of the process had just a few reminders to go with it. Students who were working on their leads, for example, could pull out this checklist and review what to keep in mind when creating them.

Teacher to Teacher | Of course, this checklist, as is the case with all tools, becomes much more effective if the teacher talks through each piece, revealing her thoughts about each topic, before asking the students to try it.

Modifying the State Performance Rubric

Teachers in Massachusetts, and around the country, are incorporating pieces of state assessments into all aspects of their curriculum. They want students to know how their work will be scored. Since the rubric used in Massachusetts is multileveled (see Figure 7.4) and could easily be overwhelming for students, we created two tools for the students to use. These tools are based on the Massachusetts rubric. Figure 7.5 illustrates our Content and Mechanics Grid and Figure 7.6 illustrates our Expository Writing Scoring Guide. Let's take a closer look at these two tools.

Content and Mechanics Grid

Barbara organized the Content and Mechanics Grid so that the students would be able to receive up to six points for content and four points for

Figure 7.3 Researching and Reporting Checklist

Part 1

Note Taking
- Read and think before you take any notes.
- Write only facts you understand.
- Write short phrases. Don't copy whole sentences from reference sources.
- Use one box on the data chart or one note card for each fact or idea.
- Include just important ideas.
- Include enough accurate information to answer the research question.

Organizing Data on a Data Chart (Marking Up the Data Chart)
- Color-code or highlight all ideas that relate to one topic with a yellow highlighter, all ideas that relate to a different topic with a pink highlighter, etc.
- Categorize related ideas—Identify all ideas that relate to one topic as #1 (1A,1B, 1C); all items that relate to a different topic as #2 (2A, 2B) etc.
- Number the ideas (1, 2, 3, 4 . . .). This is especially helpful when using the sequence text structure.

Going from Data Chart to Draft
- Read over your column headings and the notes under each heading.
- Select one column to begin your report (this does not have to be your first column).
- Use the heading of the column as the topic sentence for the paragraph.
- Determine the order of ideas or facts you want to include using the markings you made on your data chart to organize them.
- Expand the phrases you have on the data chart into complete sentences.

Part 2

Leads—Did you include . . .
- Your big question (purpose for writing the paper)?
- Interesting facts and ideas about your topic?
- Attention-grabbing sentences that make the reader want to continue to read to learn more about your topic?
- So much information that your research question is answered in the first paragraph? (I hope not.)

Transitions—Did your transitions . . .
- Help the paper flow smoothly?
- Serve as bridges between ideas?
- Help you maintain the text structure you decided to use?

Details—Do your details . . .
- Relate specifically to your topic?
- Show how much you know about your topic?
- Lead to a complete answer for your research question?

Conclusions—Did you . . .
- Decide what type of conclusion you need for your paper (summary, connect beginning to end of paper, express emotion, etc.)?
- Write a conclusion that lets the reader know that you have answered your research question and are ending the report?
- Leave off the words "The End"?

Word Choice—Did you . . .
- Avoid using the same word too many times?
- Use accurate, descriptive words?
- Use the correct words ("their," "there," "they're"; "to," "too," "two"; etc.)?

Grammar—Did your paper contain . . .
- Correct punctuation?
- Complete sentences?
- A variety of sentence types?
- Capitals where needed?
- Correct verb tense?
- Appropriate use of apostrophes?

Spelling—Did you . . .
- Proofread your work?
- Use resources to spell troublesome words?
- Think about the correct form of the word ("it's" vs. "its"; "your" vs. "you're"; "their" vs. "there")?

MCAS WRITING SCORING GUIDE (COMPOSITION)

Figure 7.4 MCAS Writing Scoring Guide (Composition)

Figure 7.4 MCAS Writing Scoring Guide (Composition)

Topic/Idea Development

1	2	3	4	5	6
• Little topic/idea development, organization, and/or details • Little or no awareness of audience and/or task	• Limited or weak topic/idea development, organization, and/or details • Limited awareness of audience and/or task	• Rudimentary topic/idea development and/or organization • Basic supporting details • Simplistic language	• Moderate topic/idea development and organization • Adequate, relevant details • Some variety in language	• Full topic/idea development • Logical organization • Strong details • Appropriate use of language	• Rich topic/idea development • Careful and/or subtle organization • Effective/rich use of language

Analytic Annotations

		Commendations		Needs
Idea Development	The overall effect of the paper	TX TY	Topic or idea development is effective and appropriate Topic or idea development is original	TJ — Topic needs more development TK — Response needs to be more appropriate to the task's requirements
Organization	The degree to which the response is • focused • clearly and logically ordered • clarified by paragraphs	OX OY OZ	Writing shows evidence of planning Writing is consistently focused from beginning to end Use of paragraphs clarifies organization and/or ideas	OJ — Ideas need to be better organized OK — Needs transitions between ideas to maintain consistent focus OL — Needs better paragraphing to clarify organization and/or ideas
Details	The degree to which the response includes examples that develop the main points	DX DY	Details are carefully chosen and relevant Details support the topic	DJ — Details are not used effectively DK — Details need to be developed instead of just listed
Language/Style	The degree to which manipulation of language, including vocabulary, word choice, word combination, and sentence variety, is effectively achieved	LX LY	Word choice adds clarity and richness Language used creates a distinctive voice, tone, or style	LJ — Needs more variety and richness in word choice LK — Sentence structure needs more variety

Standard English Conventions

1	2	3	4
• Errors seriously interfere with communication AND • Little control of sentence structure, grammar and usage, and mechanics	• Errors interfere somewhat with communication and/or • Too many errors relative to the length of the essay or complexity of sentence structure, grammar and usage, and mechanics	• Errors do not interfere with communication and/or • Few errors relative to the length of essay or complexity of sentence structure, grammar and usage, and mechanics	• Control of sentence structure, grammar and usage, and mechanics (length and complexity of essay provide opportunity for student to show control of standard English conventions)

Analytic Annotations

		Commendations		Needs
Structure	The degree to which the response includes sentences that are correct in structure	SP	Sentence structure is correct	SR — Sentence structure is not correct
Grammar and Usage	The degree to which the response demonstrates correct • use of standard grammatical rules of English • word usage and vocabulary	GP GQ	Grammatical rules are applied correctly Writing shows control of vocabulary and word usage	GR — Grammatical rules are not applied correctly GS — Words are not always used correctly
Mechanics	The degree to which the response demonstrates correct • spelling • capitalization • punctuation	MP MQ	Good use of punctuation enhances understanding Challenging words are spelled correctly	MR — Incorrect or missing punctuation interferes with understanding MS — Poor spelling interferes with communication

The Commonwealth of Massachusetts Department of Education. www.doe.mass.edu/mcas/student/2000/comp_scoring.pdf.

Figure 7.5 Content and Mechanics Grid

Page 1	1 (almost none)	2 (very little development, weak, limited)	3 (some, basic)	4 (satisfactory, adequate)	5 (much development; strong)	6 (rich, outstanding)
Organization (Paragraphs have sequence, order, and are focused)						
Details (Ideas are fully explained)						
Language/Style (Descriptive words; uses leads, transitions, etc., has voice; has sentence variety; contains figurative language)						
Topic Development (Overall impression)						

Page 2	1 (no attention paid; many errors)	2 (little attention paid; weak)	3 (basic, satisfactory, adequate)	4 (very few or no errors)
Grammar and Usage (Singular/plural agreement; no slang; consistency in verb tense)				
Mechanics (Capitalization, punctuation, and spelling)				
Sentence Structure (Overall impression)				

Figure 7.6 Expository Writing Scoring Guide

Topic/Idea Development
- presents a clear purpose for the paper
- focuses on the main purpose throughout
- develops the topic fully (not list of ideas)
- leaves the reader with a positive overall impression of the writer's knowledge of the topic

__ Extensive evidence
__ Ample evidence
__ Limited evidence
__ No evidence

Organization
- exhibits a logical sequence of ideas (beginning, middle, end)
- includes transitions that connect ideas
- ensures that the piece fits together as a whole
- displays knowledge of text structure

__ Extensive evidence
__ Ample evidence
__ Limited evidence
__ No evidence

Details
- includes details that enhance the main purpose
- chooses only details that are related to the main idea
- adds specific details to support generalizations in interesting ways
- selects details that demonstrate knowledge of the topic

__ Extensive evidence
__ Ample evidence
__ Limited evidence
__ No evidence

Language/Style (tone, voice, style)
- maintains a consistent tone that is appropriate for the purpose
- reveals the writer's own natural language (not encyclopedia)
- uses a style that captivates the reader from start to finish
- expresses ideas in an original manner

__ Extensive evidence
__ Ample evidence
__ Limited evidence
__ No evidence

Sentence Structure
- includes a variety of sentence types
- constructs sentences that are grammatically correct
- arranges sentences so they flow together smoothly

__ Extensive evidence
__ Ample evidence
__ Limited evidence
__ No evidence

Grammar/Usage
- chooses strong, accurate words
- applies rules of Standard English
- demonstrates an ability to use appropriately a wide collection of impressive words

__ Extensive evidence
__ Ample evidence
__ Limited evidence
__ No evidence

Mechanics
- uses capitals appropriately
- applies the rules of punctuation
- spells words correctly

__ Extensive evidence
__ Ample evidence
__ Limited evidence
__ No evidence

conventions, just as is the case on the Massachusetts standardized writing performance test. She created this grid in front of the students, incorporating their suggestions into its design. When students use this grid to evaluate their own work, they simply place a check in the appropriate box for each writing element. Barbara could have them jot down a brief rationale along with the checks, but instead, she chose to have them share orally some of their thinking as they score their work. Either way, this grid helps students think about the quality of their work and acknowledge what makes good writing.

Expository Writing Scoring Guide

You'll notice that we broke the Expository Writing Scoring Guide (Figure 7.6) down into the same seven elements that we used in the Content and Mechanics Grid. Again, these are the same seven elements that are addressed in the rubric designed for the Massachusetts Comprehensive Assessment System (MCAS). We included only positive descriptors in our scoring guide because we wanted our young writers to focus on what they should include in a well-written report. In creating this guide, we adapted a format that was used in a performance assessment tool developed by Schirmer and Bailey (2000) for their *Writing Assessment Rubric*. Each activity in the Schirmer and Bailey rubric was judged on "clear evidence," "some evidence," or "lack of evidence." Instead of using their three-level scale, we decided to have four levels: two levels for satisfactory reports and two levels for unsatisfactory reports. We've found that an even-numbered scale is often more telling than an odd-numbered scale. With an even-numbered scale, scorers must decide if reports are satisfactory (either 4 points or 3) or unsatisfactory (either 2 points or 1). Scorers using an odd-numbered scale can gravitate toward the center without having to make such a decision.

Assessment Rubrics Across the Country

The assessment tools we've been describing have worked well in Barbara's classroom. But today, assessment often goes well beyond the classroom. Teachers, students, parents, school boards, state departments of education and federal agencies are becoming increasingly focused on accountability and the standardization of assessment. In many states, recognition of how well students write plays a role in determining promotions, class placements, high school graduations, and funding for instructional programs. It appears that rubrics are becoming increasingly popular scoring guides. Mabry (1999) reported that thirty-eight states require state assessment programs in writing. All thirty-eight states use rubrics to score student performance. We imagine that this number has increased since the publication of Mabry's finding in 1999. Rubrics contain two essential components: (1) specific elements of writing, such as ideas, organization, sentence fluency, and mechanics; and (2) detailed descriptions of what these elements look like at different performance levels. The specific elements usually form the vertical axis of a matrix, and the descriptions form the horizontal axis.

We decided that it would be useful to know how other states assess writing performance. We wanted to make sure the strategies we're teaching align with performance standards across the country. We chose to review writing expectations from various states around the nation: Alaska, Arizona, Colorado, Florida, Georgia, Idaho, Kansas, Massachusetts, New Jersey, North Carolina, Ohio, Oregon, Pennsylvania, Rhode Island, and Wyoming. (At the end of this chapter, you'll find a list of references that will lead you to additional information about these performance assessments.)

Our analysis of state writing performance assessment instruments from these fifteen states (about one-third of the states in the country) revealed similarities and differences in how the states assess writing performance.

Some of the states (Florida, North Carolina, Rhode Island) use their rubrics to determine "focused holistic" scores. In other words, the scorers determine the overall impression of the paper while considering the traits they have identified in the rubric. Often these are narrative rubrics rather than lists of traits and descriptors. Other states—Arizona, for example—use rubrics to determine analytic scores. In this case, the scorer calculates an individual point for each trait and then averages the points to get the final score.

Several states (Alaska, Kansas, Oregon) rely on a six-point scale (or a variation of it) developed by the Northwest Regional Educational Laboratory (NREL). This rubric focuses on "ideas/content," "organization," "voice," "word choice," "sentence fluency," and "conventions." Alaska took the basic rubric from the NREL and attached to it a brief, creative, easy-to-visualize description of each element. For example, it defined "organization" as "the internal structure of the piece. It is both the skeleton and glue. Strong organization begins with a purposeful, engaging lead and wraps up with a thought-provoking close. In between, the writer takes care to link each detail or new development to a larger picture, building to a turning point or key revelation and always including strong transitions that form a kind of safety net for the reader, who never feels lost."

Interestingly, Oregon uses this same six-trait rubric from the NREL but includes an additional rubric called "citing sources." This rubric is used "only on classroom assignments requiring research." This rubric deals with plagiarism, quality of resource, documentation of citation, and so on. Isn't it nice to see attention being paid to researching?

Two-Category Rubrics: Ideas and Mechanics

As we mentioned earlier, Massachusetts divides its rubric into two broad categories: topic development and Standard English conventions. Each of these categories contain several subcategories. Up to six points may be earned for ideas and up to four points for conventions. Similarly, in Wyoming, the six-trait rubric from the NREL is divided into two broad categories as well. One category, "Expressive Skills/Content," contains purpose/voice, which is placed first in the rubric, followed by organization and then idea development. We wonder if the creators of this instrument identified "purpose and voice" first because they believe this is the most important element. We didn't notice this in any other state rubric. The second category, "Technical Skills/Mechanics," contains sentences, word choice, and conventions. The papers in Wyoming are scored analytically so that the scorer focuses on each of the six traits separately. It's interesting to consider a possible rationale for dividing the rubrics into two discrete parts. Perhaps those who designed them want to emphasize that assessing idea development needs to be detached from assessing conventions.

Rubrics: Enhancing or Inhibiting Writing?

Not everyone agrees that using rubrics to assess writing is a good thing. Mabry (1999, p. 7), for example, argues, "rubrics have the power to undermine assessment." She suggests that rubrics place too many constraints on writing by "standardizing" a process that should not be standardized. In this article, she raises serious questions about the reliability and validity of using rubrics to score high-stake state tests. Mabry refers to "rubric-driven criteria" and the "deprofessionalization" of teachers when she addresses the limited role that teachers may have in designing curriculum and instruction in situations where rubrics dominate. In an equally compelling article, Wasserstein (2001) shares her concerns about the effects of standardized testing on the writing performance of gifted students. She proposes that when teachers place too much emphasis on meeting the standards for determining exemplary achievement, they "too often impose the kind of structure that stifles and restricts thought" (p. 14). In other words, the writing becomes formulaic.

In too many classes students are taught that "good" writing consists of changing a prompt into a topic sentence, which is followed by five safe paragraphs that address the prompt. All papers end up sounding very similar. They often begin with the same sentence ("I have been asked to write about . . .") and conclude with the same sentence ("I hope you liked my paper." Or "If you want more information, you can go to the library.").

Good Writing and Standardized Tests: An Oxymoron?

From our investigation of state writing performance assessments, there is evidence to suggest that most states are working hard to ensure that teachers are not encouraging formulaic writing. The Georgia Department of

Education (2001), for example, speaks directly to this concern in a "Frequently Asked Question" sheet about test taking. Question No. 8 asks: "Is it better to play it safe, avoiding errors, or to take risks?" The response is "Content and Personal Expression are weighted more heavily than Surface Features in determining the appropriate state of writing. A well-developed, engaging paper with frequent surface feature errors will receive a higher stage score than an error free paper that lacks development and vivid language" (p. 7) (underlining in original). This document also contains ideas that teachers can use to teach writing. On page 9 are listed "Five Types of Opening Sentences" and "Five Effective Ways to End a Paper." Amazingly, these ten suggestions parallel very closely the strategies we developed. For example, one of the ideas for an opening sentence is "A question about the subject" (p. 9). This is exactly what we're after when we use our Question strategy. We are hopeful that states are nudging teachers and students to go beyond prescriptive writing on performance assessments.

The Ohio resource manual for the writing proficiency test (2000) provides another example of how a state's standards encourage students to pay attention to the craft of writing. This manual includes writing samples, annotations, and "Teaching Suggestions"—ways in which teachers can use the samples as instructional tools. The prompt for this exam asked students to write about a hero. In one of the annotations for a four-point expository paper (highest-rated), the reviewer commented, "A clear thesis [about a grandmother's influence] appears in the introduction and the conclusion effectively reconnects the grandmother to the writer's initial comment about young people's need for heroes/heroines" (p. 20). Doesn't this sound as if this student used our Connecting Beginning and End strategy?

Equally striking was another Teaching Suggestion in which students are asked to "make a list of the transitional words and sentences used in the paper. Discuss with them how transitions serve to keep readers 'on track' in a piece of writing" (p. 20). It's clear that teachers using these resources should be encouraging students to apply the strategies we've presented in order to meet the state's expectations.

We were delighted with Pennsylvania's rubric (see Figure 7.7) and the annotations that accompany the student writing samples the state releases. These annotations echo many of the strategies we have proposed and reflect our thinking completely. The annotation for a sixth-grade four-point (highest) sample read,

> This student provides the reader with an evident organizational strategy. A clear introduction ("I have strong feelings that you should keep 'Boy Meets World' on the Air"), simple and subtle transitions within and between paragraphs ("it's not just kids," "again," "finally"), and a concise conclusion ("I gave you three good reasons . . .") logically move the reader through the essay. (p. 25)

Figure 7.7 Pennsylvania Writing Assessment Domain Scoring Guide

	FOCUS	CONTENT	ORGANIZATION	STYLE	CONVENTIONS
	The single controlling point made with an awareness of task (mode) about a specific topic.	The presence of ideas developed through facts, examples, anecdotes, details, opinions, statistics, reasons and/or explanations.	The order developed and sustained within and across paragraphs using transitional devices including introduction and conclusion.	The choice, use and arrangement of words and sentence structures that create tone and voice.	The use of grammar, mechanics, spelling, usage and sentence formation.
4	Sharp, distinct controlling point made about a single topic with evident awareness of task (mode)	Substantial, specific and/or illustrative content demonstrating strong development and sophisticated ideas	Sophisticated arrangement of content with evident and/or subtle transitions	Precise, illustrative use of a variety of words and sentence structures to create consistent writer's voice and tone appropriate to audience	Evident control of grammar, mechanics, spelling, usage and sentence formation
3	Apparent point made about a single topic with sufficient awareness of task (mode)	Sufficiently developed content with adequate elaboration or explanation	Functional arrangement of content that sustains a logical order with some evidence of transitions	Generic use of a variety of words and sentence structures that may or may not create writer's voice and tone appropriate to audience	Sufficient control of grammar, mechanics, spelling, usage and sentence formation
2	No apparent point but evidence of a specific topic	Limited content with inadequate elaboration or explanation	Confused or inconsistent arrangement of content with or without attempts at transition	Limited word choice and control of sentence structures that inhibit voice and tone	Limited control of grammar, mechanics, spelling, usage and sentence formation
1	Minimal evidence of a topic	Superficial and/or minimal content	Minimal control of content arrangement	Minimal variety in word choice and minimal control of sentence structures	Minimal control of grammar, mechanics, spelling, usage and sentence formation

NON-SCORABLE

- Is illegible; i.e., includes so many indecipherable words that no sense can be made of the response
- Is incoherent; i.e., words are legible but syntax is so garbled that response makes no sense
- Is insufficient; i.e., does not include enough to assess domains adequately
- Is a blank paper

OFF-PROMPT

- Is readable but did not respond to prompt

0

Pennsylvania Department of Education. 2000–2001. Writing Assessment Handbook Supplement–Grade 6.

It seems to us that this writer employed at least two of our strategies: Right to the Point and Providing a Summary.

The annotation for the three-point paper stated,

> This student starts the essay with a simple question as an introduction ("Have you ever had to be brave at one time?") then sustains a chronologically ordered story about a football game. There is a functional conclusion ("I was so glad."). (p. 26)

Here again, we see our strategies in use. The lead is an example of Question, and the conclusion reflects the use of Sharing an Emotion.

The annotation for the two-point paper read,

> Although there is some chronological strategy present in this essay about Luke putting out the fire, the lack of connecting transitions and a weak introduction ("There was a boy") and conclusion ("He got everyone out of the house savely [sic]") detract from the progression of the story. (p. 27)

Finally, the annotation for the one-point sample read,

> There is minimal organizational strategy present in this essay about "Golden Girls," "Super Market Sweep" and Gram. The student's thoughts are random and create confusion for the reader." (p. 28)

The emphasis on effective writing is evident. There is no one correct way to answer prompts on standardized tests, no formula that has to be followed. Good writing involves a great deal more than any one blueprint can offer.

Finally, we were very impressed by the rubric used in Idaho (see Figure 7.8). If you live in Idaho, you probably already know what a five-point paper for eighth-grade expository writing looks like. According to the Idaho Department of Education, it must exhibit most of these traits:

Unique introduction which captivates reader
Satisfying conclusion
Writer establishes a purpose and maintains a clear focus
Advanced or creative approach to prompt
Effective topic sentences with supporting and/or sensory details and/or examples
Mature paragraph organization which enhances the central idea or story line
Logical development: no stray sentences or paragraphs; every part adds to whole
Thoughtful transitions: alignment, phrases, clauses, parallelism, strong sense of audience awareness
Higher-level thinking: application, analysis, and/or evaluation

Figure 7.8 Idaho Eighth-Grade Direct Writing Assessment Scoring Standard for Expository Writing

IDAHO 8TH GRADE DIRECT WRITING ASSESSMENT SCORING STANDARD FOR EXPOSITORY WRITING   Fall 1998

General Descriptions of Levels of Proficiency	5 Advanced	4 Proficient
All writing requires that the writer continuously make choices as she or he writes. The writer must ask: Who is my audience? What is my purpose? What method of development should I choose? What voice or style should I choose? Effective writers make choices and adapt their ideas, structure, and style of writing to the audience, occasion, and purpose.	A 5 paper demonstrates advanced control of the conventions of written language as well as unique qualities in style or content. A 5 paper is clear, organized, easy to understand, and characterized by a unique perspective or a mature approach to the topic. Its length is appropriate for the writer to demonstrate skills and conventions to fulfill the prompt's purpose. A score of 5 indicates that a student's writing for that particular day and prompt is clearly advanced beyond grade level.	A 4 paper demonstrates proficiency to use and understand the basic concepts of expository writing. Clear, organized, and easy to understand, a 4 paper is frequently formulaic in its development. A 4 indicates that the writer has proficient control of the conventions of written language at grade level. A score of 4 indicates that the student's writing for that particular day and prompt is proficient at grade level.
Focusing on Three Features	**5 Papers Will Exhibit MOST of the Traits Listed Below**	**4 Papers Will Exhibit MOST of the Traits Listed Below**
AUDIENCE / PURPOSE / CONTENT / ORGANIZATION These features are _most important_. Effective writing is clear, organized, interesting, and informative. Effective writers adapt their ideas, structure, and style of writing to the audience, occasion, and purpose for which they are writing. Effective writing requires that the writer continuously make choices: Who is my audience? What is my purpose? What method of development will best accomplish my purpose with my audience?	* Unique introduction which captivates reader * Satisfying conclusion * Writer establishes a purpose and maintains a clear focus * Advanced or creative approach to prompt * Effective topic sentences with supporting and/or sensory details and/or examples * Mature paragraph organization which enhances the central idea or story line * Logical development: no stray sentences or paragraphs; every part adds to whole * Thoughtful transitions: alignment, phrases, clauses, parallelism * Strong sense of audience awareness * Higher-level thinking: application, analysis, and/or evaluation	* Effective introduction (expressed or implied); may be mechanical * Evident conclusion * Evident purpose * Topic sentences with supporting details and examples rather than a list * Multiple, obvious paragraphs with continuity between them * Logical development throughout essay without stray sentences or paragraphs; every part adds to whole * Intentional transitions to connect sentences and paragraphs * Definite sense of audience awareness; anticipates and addresses reader's questions * May demonstrate higher-level thinking skills
TONE / MOOD / VOICE / STYLE These features often determine the readability of a piece of writing. Although a paper's development is appropriate for the purpose and audience, when such features are not present, the writing will likely not hold the reader's attention. Effective features may include the following literary devices which help make a piece of writing powerful, engaging, and unique: appropriate vocabulary choices, figurative language, rhythm, and parallelism.	* Powerful and engaging; holds reader's attention * Clear understanding and use of above grade-level vocabulary * Powerful verbs and precise nouns and modifiers * Reader feels strong interaction with writer and senses person behind words * Topic comes to life; writer may create new persona * Writer speaks directly to reader with an individualistic style * Confident; reader senses strong commitment to topic * Advanced use of such literary devices as personification, similes, metaphors, alliteration, allusion, irony, hyperboles, oxymorons, and understatements	* Appropriate language for audience * Interesting vocabulary which is appropriate to style * Consistent point of view, verb tense, and voice * Writes with ease and confidence; uses a natural voice * Demonstrates risk: humor or enlightenment, shows rather than tells, personal connections, dialogue, or figurative language * Varied sentences
MECHANICS / USAGE / SENTENCE STRUCTURE Eighth graders must achieve levels of standard written English which demonstrate grade level mastery of the following: spelling, capitalization, punctuation, indented paragraphing, subject-verb agreement, noun-pronoun agreement, phrases, clauses, and grammatically correct sentence structure. Compositions drafted and written within ninety minutes may not exhibit flawless language usage, mechanics, and/or sentence structure.	* Mechanically correct; may manipulate mechanics to enhance style or voice * Strong command of standard written English with few or no surface errors * Varied sentence types and structures which include complex sentences	* Mechanically correct * Few surface errors; capitalization, punctuation, and/or spelling errors do not detract from meaning or readability * Command of standard written English * Varied sentence types and structures

Note: A score of 5", 4", and 3" are considered passing; 2", 1", and 0" are not passing.

Idaho State Department of Education.

Figure 7.8 *(continued)*

IDAHO 8TH GRADE DIRECT WRITING ASSESSMENT SCORING STANDARD FOR EXPOSITORY WRITING Fall 1998

	3 Satisfactory	2 Developing	1 Minimal	0 Insufficient
	A 3 paper demonstrates a basic understanding of the organization and development of expository writing ideas. A 3 indicates that the writer has satisfactory control of the conventions of written language at grade level. Its length is appropriate for the writer to demonstrate satisfactory skills and conventions to fulfill the prompt's purpose. A score of 3 indicates that the student's writing for that particular day and prompt is satisfactory at grade level.	A 2 paper demonstrates some degree of basic expository writing skills, but is clearly flawed. A 2 paper reveals one or more of the following weaknesses: inadequate organization, inadequate development of events and details, limited or inappropriate word choices, and/or a pattern or accumulation of errors in mechanics, usage, sentence structure, or word choices. A score of 2 indicates that the student's writing for that day and prompt is developing toward satisfactory at grade level.	A 1 paper demonstrates fundamental writing deficiencies. A 1 paper contains serious and persistent writing errors, is incoherent, or is undeveloped. A score of 1 indicates that the student's writing for that day and prompt is minimal at grade level.	A 0 paper may or may not demonstrate satisfactory expository writing skills. Due to one or more traits indicated below, readers are unable to determine a final score.
	3 Papers Will Exhibit MOST of the Traits Listed Below	**2 Papers Will Exhibit MOST of the Traits Listed Below**	**1 Papers Will Exhibit MOST of the Traits Listed Below**	**0 Papers Exhibit One or More of the Traits Listed Below**
Attention to Purpose/Content/Organization	* Evident introduction * Conclusion may not effectively tie up all loose ends; reader may be left hanging * Sense of purpose * Thinking skills are appropriate to subject, audience, and purpose * Minor shifts in topic * Paragraphs work together to support whole * Limited supporting details * Redundant sentence patterns; similar beginnings * Some effective transitions help to unify essay * Awareness of audience	* Weak or ineffective introduction * Conclusion may or may not be evident * May lack sense of purpose * Shifts or changes in topic * Supporting details may be omitted or presented as a list * Disconnected paragraphs; ideas do not flow * Thought processes may be difficult to follow * Transitions may be lacking or do not unify essay * Limited awareness of audience	* Possible attempts at introduction and/or conclusion * Purpose lacks clarity or development * Inadequate organization; may display disjointed ideas * Omitted or undeveloped paragraphing; at times, may be so frequent that it has no relationship to organization * Difficult-to-follow thought processes * Text may be repetitious and/or contain random thoughts * Demonstrates lack of understanding of audience and purpose	* Blank * Illegible * Too brief to assess * Written in language other than English * Written using medium other than blue or black ink * Written to topic other than specified in prompt * Written in form other than expository essay
Tone/Voice/Mood/Verb/Style	* Seemingly sincere, but not fully engaged or involved in writing * Appropriate vocabulary; may be mechanical or quite general * Variety of verb choices * Generally consistent point of view, verb tense, and voice; occasional drifting * Moments of enlightenment—reader longs to learn more * Attempts to use colorful language; may include jargon or clichés * Does not overuse I	* Simplistic style: too frequent use of I; passive and/or simplistic verbs; frequent use of would and could; few precise nouns and specific modifiers * Limited vocabulary * Inappropriate or ineffective word choices * Inconsistent or inappropriate voice	* Restricted vocabulary: inadequate word pool; lacks language development; inadequate word choices * Language errors leave reader wondering what message writer is attempting to convey * Overuse of such connectives as and, and so, but then, and then, and because * Monotonous or lifeless voice * Requires rereading for understanding; message may be vague	
Mechanics/s/Usage/S/Sentence structure	* Most surface errors do not detract from meaning and/or readability * Some short, unvaried sentences * Correct end punctuation; some correct internal punctuation * Correctly uses and spells such priority words as the following: their, they're, to, two, too, your, you're, its, it's, then, than, which, witch, and a lot * Infrequent nonstandard sentence structure * Evident paragraphing	* Surface errors detract from meaning and readability * Few spelling errors in common words * Errors in punctuation require rereading for clarity and/or understanding * Correct ending punctuation; missing or incorrect internal punctuation * Patterns of short, simple sentences * Choppy and/or awkward sentences * Fragmented and/or run-on sentences * Attempted paragraphing * Too frequent connectives	* Glaring surface errors detract from meaning and readability * Indistinguishable sentences * Poor and/or incorrect word usage * Misuse and/or little use of capitalization and punctuation * Frequently omitted or incorrect internal and terminal punctuation * Requires rereading due to word usage and/or punctuation errors * Frequent spelling errors, including misspellings of common words * Little or no separation of paragraphs	

This is a comprehensive description of good writing. Our challenge as teachers is to make sure students know how to apply this description, or other thoughtful descriptions, to their work. We couldn't help but smile when we read Mabry's (1999) quote: "You can weigh the calf as much as you want, but it won't grow unless you feed it." How true. Likewise, we can't expect students' writing to improve by merely assessing it; we need to teach them skills and strategies first. Linking assessment and instruction provides us with opportunities to make this happen.

☑ Checking In with Nick

Before we conclude, let's visit with Nick one last time. We'll use our Expository Writing Scoring Guide to evaluate his final paper (see Figure 7.9). See if you agree with our assessment. We've also provided a rationale for the performance level we gave Nick for each trait.

Certain to Survive?

It's newborn body weighs only 2 oz., but eventually it will eat about 30 pounds of food each day. Who could eat this much food? An African elephant? A Great White Shark? Nope. The one with the big appetite is the cuddly panda.

You may be wondering where they get all this food. Actually, they eat mostly bamboo, which can be found only in southwest China. It's sad to say that only about 1,000 of them live in the wild and another 100 live in zoos around the world. Why are there so few and what are people doing to protect them?

A long time ago, hunters killed pandas for their fur. It was used for rugs. The pandas had thick fur that kept them warm in their cold weather.

When Pandas were first discovered, they were killed so scientists could study their skin and bones. They were trying to learn more about them. They knew they looked sort of like bears but they didn't hibernate like bears and they can't walk on their hind legs. Also, pandas can grab onto bamboo easily because one of their bones in their wrists is larger and longer than the others. They also have strong jaws and strong teeth witch helps them eat the hard bamboo. If you was a scientist wouldn't you want to find out about all these unique things about pandas too?

Another reason there are so few pandas is because people have built homes and farms in the mountain valleys of China where pandas used to live. The pandas had to move up into the colder mountains to get food and water. This was not good because they ran out of their food supply and because they had to live closer to men who could kill them.

Today the Chinese government is protecting pandas and their land. It's now against the law to kill them and officials plant bamboo so pandas always have enough food.

Figure 7.9 Expository Writing Scoring Guide—Nick's Assessment

Topic/Idea Development
- presents a clear purpose for the paper
- focuses on the main purpose throughout
- develops the topic fully (not list of ideas)
- leaves the reader with a positive overall impression of the writer's knowledge of the topic

___ Extensive evidence
✓ Ample evidence
___ Limited evidence
___ No evidence

Organization
- exhibits a logical sequence of ideas (beginning, middle, end)
- includes transitions that connect ideas
- ensures that the piece fits together as a whole
- displays knowledge of text structure

___ Extensive evidence
✓ Ample evidence
___ Limited evidence
___ No evidence

Details
- includes details that enhance the main purpose
- chooses only details that are related to the main idea
- adds specific details to support generalizations in interesting ways
- selects details that demonstrate knowledge of the topic

___ Extensive evidence
✓ Ample evidence
___ Limited evidence
___ No evidence

Language/Style (tone, voice, style)
- maintains a consistent tone that is appropriate for the purpose
- reveals the writer's own natural language (not encyclopedia)
- uses a style that captivates the reader from start to finish
- expresses ideas in an original manner

___ Extensive evidence
✓ Ample evidence
___ Limited evidence
___ No evidence

Sentence Structure
- includes a variety of sentence types
- constructs sentences that are grammatically correct
- arranges sentences so they flow together smoothly

___ Extensive evidence
✓ Ample evidence
___ Limited evidence
___ No evidence

Grammar/Usage
- chooses strong, accurate words
- applies rules of Standard English
- demonstrates an ability to use appropriately a wide collection of impressive words

___ Extensive evidence
✓ Ample evidence
___ Limited evidence
___ No evidence

Mechanics
- uses capitals appropriately
- applies the rules of punctuation
- spells words correctly

___ Extensive evidence
✓ Ample evidence
___ Limited evidence
___ No evidence

Although man has killed lots of pandas in the past now people everywhere want to help pandas. Pandas have been brought to zoos where zookeepers give them vitamins and put them on special diets to keep them healthy. Sometimes they live in dark, air-conditioned sections of the zoo, so they feel like they are at home in the mountains of

China. Pandas like to be near water, so zookeepers make sure they have plenty to use for drinking, playing and cooling off. Pandas who live in the wild usually live about 15 years. Pandas who live in captivity can live into their 20s.

No matter if the pandas live in China or in a zoo, it seems that everyone is now working hard to make sure they live long, safe lives. Perhaps this will help keep pandas from becoming extinct so people in years to come can also enjoy these cuddly-looking animals.

Rationale for Scores

- Nick's purpose is stated at the end of the second paragraph. With a bit more idea development we would have rated it "extensive evidence."
- The paper seems to be organized in a way that it moves the reader along from one piece of evidence to the next. It has a beginning, middle, and end. We can tell that he used the Explanation text structure. Nick stays focused on the topic.
- He used some transitions that moved the reader from idea to idea. Although they were effective, they didn't add a great deal of excitement to the piece.
- Perhaps the biggest weakness of this paper is that not all supporting details are developed fully, but they do enhance the main purpose of his report, are relevant, and do demonstrate his knowledge of the panda's plight.
- Nick's vocabulary was not extensive, but the words he chose were accurately used and correctly spelled for the most part.

As we noted earlier, the writing samples in the Ohio test manual (2000) are accompanied by "Teaching Suggestions." This feature was extremely useful for us, so we decided to include some possible follow-up activities for you and your students to try with Nick's report.

Follow-up Activities

- Ask students to identify how Nick made the transition from the first paragraph to the second. What word linked the two paragraphs?
- Look back through your folder of strategies for leads and conclusions. Which strategy did Nick use for the lead? for the conclusion?
- In a large group, ask students to identify the main purpose of this report. In which paragraph did you find out this purpose? Together, make a list of the evidence Nick uses to support his purpose for writing this report.
- Get with a partner. Make a list of specific ways in which Nick could have left the reader with a more positive overall impression of his knowledge of pandas. Find other relevant facts about pandas and revise this draft to include them.

Nick has achieved a great deal in a short few weeks. He's learned how to generate big research questions, collect data, organize information, and write a report that demonstrates his content knowledge, follows a logical progression of ideas, and answers a question that was important to Nick. This paper reflects Nick's voice and person. What more could we ask for?

Throughout this process, we've learned many things. Perhaps the most important is that there's no end to what students can accomplish once they know how to craft expository pieces that convey important information in engaging ways.

State Writing Performance Assessments

Alaska
Fenton, R., T. Straugh, and F. Stofflet. 1997. Alaska Writing Assessment—1997: Preliminary Technical Report. Paper presented at the Standards in Action Forum of the Alaska State Department of Education, Anchorage, Alaska (ERIC Document Reproduction Service No. ED 414312).

Arizona
Arizona's Instrument to Measure Standards—Writing. Retrieved December 19, 2001, from www.ade.state.az.us/

Colorado
Colorado Student Assessment Program: 1997 Demonstration Booklet, Grade 4 Reading and Writing. Colorado State Department of Education, Denver (ERIC Document Reproduction Service No. ED 409529).

Florida
Florida Writes: Report on the 1999 Assessment, Grade 4 Florida Writing Assessment Program. Florida State Department of Education, Tallahassee (ERIC Document Reproduction Service No. ED 436564).

Georgia
Georgia Department of Education Writing Assessment. Retrieved December 14, 2001, from www.doe.k12.ga.us/sla/ret/writing.html

Idaho
Idaho Department of Education Bureau of Curriculum and Accountability—Statewide testing. Retrieved January 4, 2002, from www.sde.state.id.us/instruct/Statewidetest.htm

Kansas
Kansas Writing Assessment. Retrieved December 27, 2001, from www.bluevalleyk12.org/ca/testing/assessment_kwa.htm

Massachusetts
MCAS Writing Scoring Guide (Long Composition). Massachusetts Department of Education, Massachusetts Comprehensive Assessment System. Retrieved February 17, 2002, from www.doe.mass.edu/mcas/student/2001/

New Jersey
New Jersey Professional Education Port, Language Arts Literacy Test Specifications. Retrieved January 4, 2002, from http://njpep.rutgers.edu/TestSpecs/LangArts/Scoring/RubricsNJwritingESPA.html

North Carolina
Report of Student Performance in Writing, 1998–1999, Grades 4, 7, and 10. North Carolina Testing Program (ERIC Document Reproduction Service No. ED 432768).

Ohio
The Ninth-Grade Proficiency Test in Writing: A Resource Manual for Teachers of Writing. Ohio Department of Education, Columbus (ERIC Document Reproduction Service No. ED 443122).

Oregon
Scoring Guides, Oregon Department of Education. Retrieved December 9, 2001, from www.ode.state.or.us/asmt/resource/scorguides/

Pennsylvania
The Pennsylvania State Assessment System, Supplemental Documentation for 1999 Reading, Mathematics and Writing Assessment Reports. Retrieved December 27, 2001, from www.pde.psu.edu

Rhode Island
Writing Assessment: Rhode Island State Assessment Program, Guide to Interpretation [and] Interpretation Guide for Families Grades 3, 7, and 10. Rhode Island State Department of Education, Providence (ERIC Document Reproduction Service No. ED 438293).

Wyoming
WyCAS On-Demand Writing Scoring Guide. Retrieved December 27, 2001, from www.measuredprogress.org/wycas/Testdsgn/WritingRubric1.html

Using Nonfiction Picture Books to Model Expository Writing Strategies

Transitions

1. Repeat a Word

Darling, T., and K. Darling. 1996. *How to Babysit an Orangutan*. New York: Walker. (see "job," p. 7)

Hirschi, R. 2000. *Octopuses*. Minneapolis, MN: Carolrhoda Books. (see "predators," pp. 29–30)

St. George, J. 2000. *So You Want to Be President?* New York: Philomel Books. (see "general," p. 34)

2. Use Related Words

Dingle, D. T. 1998. *First in the Field: Baseball Hero Jackie Robinson*. New York: Hyperion Books. (see "church"—"house of worship," p. 11)

Greenberg, D. 2000. *Chimpanzees*. New York: Benchmark Books. (see "human beings"—"people," p. 36)

Markle, S. 1997. *Outside and Inside Bats*. New York: Atheneum Books. (see "small fruit"—"food," p. 25)

3. End Paragraph with a Question

Armstrong, J. 1998. *Shipwreck at the Bottom of the World*. New York: Crown. (p. 2)

Branley, F. M. 1986. *What the Moon Is Like*. New York: Thomas Y. Crowell. (p. 5)

Maslin, M. 2000. *Storm*. Austin, TX: Raintree Steck-Vaughn. (p. 4)

4. Begin a Paragraph with a Question

Harness, C. 2000. *George Washington*. Washington, DC: National Geographic Society. (p. 15)

St. George, J. 2000. *So You Want to Be President?* New York: Philomel Books. (pp. 22, 26)

Schmandt-Besserat, D. 1999. *The History of Counting.* New York: Morrow Junior Books. (pp. 10, 20, 24, 26, 34)

5. Contrast

Darling, K. 1996. *Rain Forest Babies.* New York: Walker. ("Unlike a human baby . . ." see "Sloth")

Darling, K. 2000. *There's a Zoo on You!* Brookfield, CT: The Millbrook Press. ("Unlike most microbes, the lactobacillus . . .," p. 38)

Greenberg, D. 2000. *Chimpanzees.* New York: Benchmark Books. ("On the other hand," p. 8)

Oleksy, W. 2000. *The Philippines: Enchantment of the World.* New York: Children's Press. ("Contrasting with the . . .," p. 113)

St. George, J. 2000. *So You Want to Be President?* New York: Philomel Books. (pp. 10, 34, 41 [e.g., "Presidents Who Were Honest, Presidents Who Were Not Honest"; "good things, bad things"])

6. "Although"

George, M. 2000. *Wolves.* The Child's World®. (p. 8)

Darling, K. 1996. *Rain Forest Babies.* New York: Walker. (see "Sugar Glider")

Maestro, B. 2000. *Struggle for a Continent: The French and Indian Wars 1689–1763.* New York: HarperCollins. (pp. 12, 24)

7. "Is Another"

Hirschi, R. 2000. *Octopuses.* Minneapolis, MN: Carolrhoda Books. (pp. 20–21, 23)

Hughes, M. S. 2000. *Flavor Foods: Spices and Herbs.* Minneapolis, MN: Lerner Publications. (p. 77)

St. George, J. 2000. *So You Want to Be President?* New York: Philomel Books (p. 37)

8. Appositive

Freedman, R. 2000. *Give Me Liberty: The Story of the Declaration of Independence.* New York: Holiday House. (p. 26, used in two places)

Grace, C. O. 1999. *I Want to Be a Firefighter.* New York: Harcourt Brace. (p. 28)

Hughes, M. S. 2000. *Flavor Foods: Spices and Herbs.* Minneapolis, MN: Lerner Publications. (p. 80)

9. Several to One

Harris, A., and P. Weissman. 1990. *The Great Voyager Adventure: A Guided Tour Through the Solar System.* Englewood Cliffs, NJ: Simon & Schuster.

10. Back and Forth

Markle, S. 1996. *Outside and Inside Sharks.* New York: Atheneum Books for Young Readers. (pp. 27–28, 34–35)

11. Command

Grupper, J. 1997. *Destination: Rainforest*. Washington, DC: National Geographic Society. (p. 4)

Markle, S. 1996. *Outside and Inside Spiders*. New York: Bradbury Press. (p. 13)

Markle, S. 1997. *Outside and Inside Bats*. New York: Atheneum Books. (pp. 6–7, 10–12)

12. Same Start

Markle, S. 1997. *Outside and Inside Bats*. New York: Atheneum Books. (pp. 20–21)

Oleksy, W. 2000. *The Philippines: Enchantment of the World*. New York: Children's Press. (p. 29)

Vogt, G. L. 2000. *Pluto*. Mankato, MN: Bridgestone Books. (p. 17)

Leads

1. Question

Darling, T., and K. Darling. 1996. *How to Babysit an Orangutan*. New York: Walker. (p. 1)

George, M. 2000. *Wolves*. The Child's World®. (p. 1)

Budiansky, S. 2000. *The World According to Horses: How They Run, See, and Think*. New York: Henry Holt. (p. 77) This is not exactly a picture book, but it does contain pictures and diagrams. Appropriate for more accomplished readers or readers who have background knowledge of horses.

2. "Imagine"

Markle, S., and W. Markle. 1998. *Gone Forever: An Alphabet of Extinct Animals*. New York: Atheneum Books. (see "Elephant Bird" and "Captain Maclear's Rat")

Silver, D. M. 1994. *One Small Square, African Savanna*. New York: W. H. Freeman. (p. 6)

Armstrong, J. 1998. *Shipwreck at the Bottom of the World*. New York: Crown. (p. 1)

3. Guess Who or What?

Darling, K. 1996. *Rain Forest Babies*. New York: Walker. (see "Orangutan")

Badt, K. L. 1994. *Hair There and Everywhere*. New York: Children's Press. (p. 4)

4. Common Reaction

Markle, S., and W. Markle. 1998. *Gone Forever: An Alphabet of Extinct Animals*. New York: Atheneum Books. ("Dodo Bird")

Gibbons, G. 1999. *Pigs*. New York: Holiday House. (p. 1)

Hinds, K. 2001. *Hamsters and Gerbils*. New York: Benchmark Books. (p. 9)

5. Right to the Point

Travers, W. 2000. *Elephant*. Austin, TX: Raintree Steck-Vaughn. (see "Threats," p. 38)

Corey, S. 2000. *You Forgot Your Skirt, Amelia Bloomer!* New York: Scholastic. (p. 1)

Lutz, N. J. 2001. *Frederick Douglass: Abolitionist and Author.* Philadelphia: Chelsea House. (p. 7)

6. Series of Intriguing Questions

Grace, C. O. 1999. *I Want to Be a Firefighter.* New York: Harcourt Brace. (p. 6)

Goodman, S. E. 2001. *Ultimate Field Trip: Blasting Off to Space Academy.* New York: Atheneum Books for Young Readers. (p. 1)

Ride, S., and T. O'Shaughnessy. 1999. *The Mystery of Mars.* New York: Crown. This two-page lead ends with a series of intriguing questions.

7. Question and Two-Word Questions

This strategy was designed by Chloe, a fifth grader. We haven't seen it used in picture books, but we think it's a wonderful way for some nonfiction to begin.

8. Hanging On

Collard, S. B. III. 1992. *Do They Scare You? Creepy Creatures.* Watertown, MA: Charlesbridge. (see "Giant Squid")

Greenberg, D. 2000. *Chimpanzees.* New York: Benchmark Books. (p. 5)

Walker, S. M. 1999. *Sea Horses.* Minneapolis, MN: Carolrhoda Books. (p. 6)

9. Past to Present

Oleksy, W. 2000. *The Philippines: Enchantment of the World.* New York: Children's Press. (pp. 13, 41)

Schafer, S. 1999. *Turtles.* New York: Benchmark Books. (p. 11)

10. Indisputable Fact

Furniss, T. 2001. *Spinning Through Space: The Sun.* Austin, TX: Raintree Steck-Vaughn. (see "Spacecraft Explorers," p. 24)

Grace, C. O. 1999. *I Want to Be a Firefighter.* New York: Harcourt Brace. (p. 6)

Travers, W. 2000. *Elephant.* Austin, TX: Raintree Steck-Vaughn. (p. 4)

11. What's Wrong?

Green, J. 1999. *Endangered! Butterflies.* New York: Benchmark Books. (p. 20)

Jackson, D. M. 2000. *The Wildlife Detectives: How Forensic Scientists Fight Crimes Against Nature.* Boston: Houghton Mifflin. (p. 4)

12. Anecdote

January, B. 1999. *Science in the Renaissance.* New York: Grolier. (p. 21)

Patent, D. H. 1996. *Biodiversity*. New York: Clarion Books. (p. 77)
Pinkney, A. D. 2000. *Let It Shine: Stories of Black Women Freedom Fighters.* San Diego: Gulliver Books/Harcourt. (see "Mary McLeod Bethune," p. 39)

13. Inside Someone's Head
Stevens, J. 1995. *From Pictures to Words: A Book About Making a Book.* New York: Holiday House. In this picture book, author-illustrator Janet Stevens is having a conversation with the imaginary characters in her head. The whole book comes from Inside Someone's Head.

14. What's Being Done?
Grace, C. O. 1999. *I Want to Be a Firefighter.* New York: Harcourt Brace. (p. 33)

15. Paradox
Markle, S. 1995. *Outside and Inside Snakes.* New York: Macmillan. (p. 3)

Combining Strategies

"Imagine" plus Series of Questions
Hirschi, R. 2000. *Octopuses*. Minneapolis, MN: Carolrhoda Books. (p. 10)

Right to the Point plus Series of Questions
Markle, S. 1996. *Outside and Inside Sharks.* New York: Atheneum. (p. 3)

Conclusions

1. Dreaming of the Future
Branley, F. M. 1986. *What the Moon Is Like.* New York: Thomas Y. Crowell. (pp. 30–31)
Cerullo, M. M. 2000. *The Truth About the Great White Shark.* San Francisco: Chronicle Books. (p. 40)
Simon, S. 2000. *Gorillas*. New York: HarperCollins. (last page)

2. Posing a Question
Collard, S. B. III. 1992. *Do They Scare You? Creepy Creatures.* Watertown, MA: Charlesbridge. (see "Gulpers and Viper Fish")
Corey, S. 2000. *You Forgot Your Skirt, Amelia Bloomer!* New York: Scholastic. (last page)

3. Ask a Question and Answer It
Collard, S. B. III. 1992. *Do They Scare You? Creepy Creatures.* Watertown, MA: Charlesbridge. (last paragraph)

Swinburne, S. R. 1999. *Once a Wolf: How Wildlife Biologists Fought to Bring Back the Gray Wolf.* Boston: Houghton Mifflin. (p. 28)

Zoehfeld, K. W. 1999. *Dinosaur Babies.* New York: HarperCollins. (p. 31)

4. "Although"

Bial, R. 2001. *The Apache.* New York: Benchmark Book. (p. 99)

Darling, T., and K. Darling. 1996. *How to Babysit an Orangutan.* New York: Walker. (p. 32)

January, B. 1999. *Science in the Renaissance.* New York: Grolier. (p. 47)

5. "Finally"

Greenberg, D. 2000. *Chimpanzees.* New York: Benchmark Books. (p. 11)

Markle, S., and W. Markle. 1998. *Gone Forever: An Alphabet of Extinct Animals.* New York: Atheneum Books. (see "Barbary Lion")

Schmandt-Besserat, D. 1999. *The History of Counting.* New York: Morrow Junior Books. (p. 41)

6. "Help!

Green, J. 1999. *Endangered! Butterflies.* New York: Benchmark Books. (pp. 26–29)

Thapar, V. 2001. *Tiger.* Austin, TX: Raintree Steck-Vaughn. (pp. 42–43)

7. No Doubt About It!

Dyer, A. 1999. *Space.* New York: Reader's Digest Children's Books. (p. 60)

Koscielniak, B. 2000. *The Story of the Incredible Orchestra.* Boston: Houghton Mifflin. (last sentence begins with "Without a doubt . . .")

8. Giving Advice

Machotka, H. 1992. *Breathtaking Noses.* New York: Morrow Junior Books. (last page)

Schafer, S. 1999. *Turtles.* New York: Benchmark Books. (pp. 28–29)

Stevens, J. 1995. *From Pictures to Words: A Book About Making a Book.* New York: Holiday House. (last page)

9. Sharing an Emotion

Darling, K. 1996. *Rain Forest Babies.* New York: Walker. (last page "About the Rain Forests")

Hinds, K. 2001. *Hamsters and Gerbils.* New York: Benchmark Books. (p. 29)

10. What's Next?

Maestro, B. 2000. *Struggle for a Continent: The French and Indian Wars 1689–1763.* New York: HarperCollins. (p. 45)

Stefoff, R. 2001. *Utah.* New York: Benchmark Books. (p. 85)

Vogt, G. L. 2000. *Pluto.* Mankato, MN: Bridgestone Books. (p. 26)

11. Right Now

Ammon, R. 2000. *Conestoga Wagons*. New York: Holiday House. (last page)

Grace, C. O. 1999. *I Want to Be a Firefighter*. New York: Harcourt Brace. (pp. 29, 31)

January, B. 1999. *Science in the Renaissance*. New York: Grolier. (p. 58)

12. "No Matter" Plus Draw a Conclusion

We couldn't find examples of this strategy in picture books, but it works well for shorter reports.

13. Providing a Summary

George, M. 2000. *Wolves*. The Child's World®. (p. 31)

St. George, J. 2000. *So You Want to Be President?* New York: Philomel Books. (p. 47)

Simon, S. 1993. *Autumn Across America*. New York: Hyperion Books. (last page)

14. Connecting Beginning and End

George, M. 2000. *Wolves*. The Child's World®. (pp. 7, 31)

Jordan, B. 2000. *Lion*. Austin, TX: Raintree Steck-Vaughn. (pp. 4, 43)

Markle, S. 1996. *Outside and Inside Sharks*. New York: Atheneum Books. (pp. 5, 35)

15. Quote

Giblin, J. C. 1983. *Fireworks, Picnics, and Flags: The Story of the Fourth of July Symbols*. New York: Clarion Books. (p. 11)

Pinkney, A. D. 2000. *Let It Shine: Stories of Black Women Freedom Fighters*. San Diego: Gulliver Books/Harcourt. (see "Mary Mcleod Bethune," p. 49)

Stefoff, R. 2001. *Nevada*. New York: Benchmark Books. (pp. 51, 117)

Using Technology to Enhance Researching and Writing

Thoughts About Technology

Technology is a gateway to better writing. Word processing functions make it much easier to revise work, to improve leads and transitions, and to add figurative language. They give writers tools to enhance their work.

Technology also provides a strong base on which to build the research process. With so much information out there, the researcher has a means to access that knowledge. Books alone do not educate the learner for today and tomorrow's society.

Writing the First Draft

Some teachers prefer to have students handwrite their first draft because of their lack of keyboarding skills. It is agonizing and a waste of time to watch students pick out one letter at a time. However, future drafts should be put on a word processor for easier revisions. For the "one letter at a time pecker," volunteers such as parents or senior citizens can help input student work exactly as it is written into the computer. Work can be saved in a text format so that disks can travel back and forth between school and home regardless of whether computers are Macintosh or Windows based. Students with access to e-mail can send drafts between home and school.

For those who don't have access to computers, keyboarding devices like AlphaSmarts are extremely helpful. These portable keyboards are so lightweight that they can travel effortlessly. Students can easily download and save their work into a word processing application. Software is now available for AlphaSmarts that will allow the user to transfer files from the computer to this keyboard device.

How to Save Older Drafts

Students can save drafts of their work to show the progress they've made in revising it. In order to save the drafts, students need to understand the differences between "save" and "save as." Having a large-screen monitor hooked up to the computer to teach this is extremely helpful. For this whole-class lesson, a demonstration using Nick's panda report might look like this:

> In the student folder, open Nick's first draft that is labeled Nickpanda#1. Immediately, Nick should do a SAVE AS before any changes are made. Nick should title this file Nickpanda#2. When changes are made on this second draft, Nick would just hit the SAVE key. Nick now has two files: Nickpanda#1 (his original) and Nickpanda#2 (with revisions). When Nick is ready to make more changes, he will open Nickpanda#2 and immediately do a SAVE AS and call this file Nickpanda#3. As previously, Nick should then hit save when he has completed his revisions for Nickpanda #3. These same procedures can be followed for all additional drafts. In this way, students and teachers can assess progress as strategies are taught.

Not Enough Computers?

For classrooms without sufficient computers, teachers need to be creative to way find ways to maximize computer use within the room. They also need to be resourceful in accessing computers outside the classroom. Ideally, schools would have computer laboratories and enough computers and portable keyboard devices with a high student ratio within each classroom, but in reality that rarely happens.

In a typical classroom, students can print out drafts on which to make revisions. While other students are on computers, students can confer with classmates and receive feedback from one another. If portable keyboard devices are available, they can also use them to work on their revisions.

For accessing computers outside the classroom that are not being used, students need to be supervised. In these cases, support staff and volunteers can be extremely valuable. Often support professionals welcome this opportunity to work with their targeted students. Perhaps the librarian might be willing to monitor students using computers when there are no classes. If a school is fortunate to have a computer laboratory, some machines might be free while classes are being held. Volunteers can accompany students. If another classroom is available (for example, its students might be at lunch or with a specialist), volunteers could also monitor students using these computers. By engaging others to buy into your project from the very beginning, you can use them as resources to increase your technological resources.

Tips on Organizing Student Files—For Single Classes

1. On the desktop, create a new folder and call it Research Project.
2. Within this Research folder, create a folder for each student. Label it with the student name.
3. Have students save all their work in their individual folders.
4. Make sure students date and/or label all their research files.

Tips on Organizing Student Files—For Multiple Classes

1. On the desktop, create new folders for each class. Label them by the title of the class.
2. Within each class folder, create a folder for each student. Label it with the student name.
3. Continue with the same steps as above.

Tips on Downloading Portable Keyboards

1. Students should be independent in this process. They should train one another and build up a cadre of "experts" available to help.
2. Set up a system for downloading with the class. Schedule times throughout the day for downloading. For example, some may do it first thing when they come in; others may wait to midmorning.
3. Make sure students label and save their work in their own files.

Tips for Accessing Drafts of Student Files

1. If computers in the classroom are networked, files can be sent from one to another in the room.
2. If there is a computer lab, copy research folders with student work onto the server. When students go to the computer lab, they can then open their files on their research.
3. If there is e-mail, files can be sent as attachments to other computers that also have e-mail capabilities in and outside of the classroom.

How to Find Age-Level Material

It's very difficult to make a permanent list of useful research sites because the Internet is so rapidly changing. Sites that may be valuable resources for one project may not even exist the next time visited. There are reputable resources that do list sites for various grade levels. Electronic resources such as online encyclopedias may be geared to different age groups. For example, Grolier Online contains various references geared to age levels. Their New Book of Knowledge is geared to younger students. Others such as government sites may also organize material by age. For example, NASA has resources developed for younger students on its StarChild site (http://starchild.gsfc.nasa.gov/docs/StarChild/StarChild.html). Some sites, which carry awards for children, may also be a benchmark of their appropriateness. Be careful with organizations and universities, as material may be too difficult to understand. Like buying anything, go somewhere reputable such as The Discovery Channel (www.discovery.com), the Exploratorium (www.exploratorium.edu) or National Geographic (www.nationalgeographic.com). Students need to understand that reputable sites will likely contain more accurate information.

Teaching Strategies

Spend time with students doing whole-class lessons with the computer hooked up to the monitor on devising strategies to locate materials. Some students have already developed successful methods to find resources and will be able to share these with their classmates. Explain how to make a site a favorite or how to bookmark it. Demonstrate how students can e-mail pages to their homes if they have access to the Internet, since many will want to continue their research at home. Provide lessons on how to copy selected passages (and, of course, giving credit) into a word processing application rather than printing out the entire article.

Internet Precautions

1. Monitor students on Internet use. Students should be supervised even if there are filters. Discuss what to do if an inappropriate site does come up.
2. Use parents and other volunteers for supervisions. Make arrangements for them to have some kind of training about their role before or after school.

Student Reports

Grade 4: Lynette's Book Report

Lynette and her classmates were asked to write nonfiction book reports. Lynette's report, however, illustrates how she applies some of the strategies, especially those for transitions.

Penguins

This book is about penguins. In this book it tells about what penguins eat, what they build there nests out of and how they survive in all conditions. Penguins eat all different kinds of foods. [*Lynette attempted to use Several to One to make the transition between these two paragraphs.*]

Penguins like to eat food from the water. They eat many kinds of food. Fish is always on the penguins' menu. Penguins will always eat fish. Fish is the penguins favorite food. Penguins eat other foods too! The other foods that penguins eat are squid, krill, and crustaceans. Most penguins eat in the same way but Adelie penguins have a special way of feeding their babies. The special way they feed their babies is from a pocket in their mouth. Do you know where baby penguins are fed and raised? [*Here, Lynette uses End a Paragraph with a Question to transition to the next paragraph. As you read this paragraph, notice all the ways Lynette transitions between sentences.*]

Different kinds of penguins make different kinds of nests. This is because they use what is in their habitat to make their nests. For example, Black-footed penguins make nests. To build their nests, black-footed penguins use vegetation, feathers, and/or stones. Another example is when Gentoo penguins make their nests. They dig holes and line them with grass. Then the male and female take turns keeping the eggs farm.

Finally Rock hopper penguins build there nests by digging a hole and lining it partly with rocks. Penguin babies can survive in the cold weather of Antartica. [*Lynette uses Back and Forth as she moves the reader from one idea to the next in these two paragraphs.*]

Survival is important to the penguins. Not all penguins survive to be an old penguin. Before the baby penguin is born its in it's mommy's warm body That means that when they are born they are helpless and cold because Antartica is cold. When penguns are born they have no feathers. The penguins keep warm from layers of insulation. Another way penguins stay warm is from over lapping feathers and oil that makes a waterproof suit. [*Notice the way Lynette uses Contrast to connect these two paragraphs.*]

One thing penguins can't survive is oil spills. How the penguins die from oil spills is that first there feathers get soaked in oil and can't protect them from the cold. Then when the penguins try to get the oil of the oil poisons them. Millions of penguins die from oil spills every year.

I think it was interesting to learn about penguins. They are very unusual animals. [*Lynette has demonstrated her understanding about transitions. The next step will be for Lynette to learn some strategies to use in revising her lead and conclusion. Her report will also be more fluid as she combines shorter sentences.*]

Grade 5: Kathryn's Science Research Report

How Did the Universe Start?

Imagine you are way, way, way, way back in time, before people, before dinosaurs, before the earth and stars, even before the universe. You are in a cloud of nothing. It is so very hot, especially near this fireball of some sort. You don't know what it is or what it is going to do, and all of a sudden, BANG! Scientists today are studying this and all the while, we are waiting for an answer to "How did the universe start?" I've wondered about this question when I lookup into the night sky. [*Kathryn uses the "Imagine" strategy as her lead. Next, she transitions with Repeat a Related Word: "universe start" in the first paragraph and "the origin of the universe" in the second.*]

Scientists have many theories about the origin of the universe, but the most common one is the Big Bang Theory. Why is that? For one thing, it explains why the universe is always expanding and why it seems so uniform in all places and directions. With the evidence that is currently available and the discovery of background radiation to substantiate it, the Big Bang theory appears to be the best account for the evolution of the universe. The Cosmic Background Explorer (COBE) accurately measured the background radiation from 1989–1993. They subtracted radiation from the sky from known sources. Background radiation was set free from a change of hydrogen atoms that absorbed wavelengths of light. The formation of atoms allowed other wavelengths of light which interfered with free electrons that set free radiation that we are able to detect today. This has revealed that the background radiation fits the predictions of the Big Bang so accurately that scientists considered the Big Bang to be the correct explanation of the beginning of the universe. [*Kathryn connects these two paragraphs by continuing the idea of the big bang theory and using the word "also."*]

The Big Bang theory also seeks the explanation of what really happened at or soon after the beginning of the universe. The Big Bang has a lot to it, like the universe being packed into the fireball. How was the universe compressed into the fireball? If the universe is much bigger today than billions of years ago, everything was much smaller before the Big Bang. In this way, objects were able to fit in the fireball. Also, billions of years ago, the existing heat, gas, and density might have somehow caused the universe to be smaller to fit in the fireball. After being packed into the fireball for so long, the main part of our Big Bang theory occurred. The explosion! [*What a clever transition. Kathryn combines two strategies: Repeat a Word and Begin a Paragraph with a Question.*]

What explosion? Thousands and thousands of years ago, a man named George Gamow and his students developed an idea of a hot explosion of matter and energy at the origin of the universe. They also hypothesized that remains of the Big Bang explosion may still be circulating in the universe. Before the explosion, the universe was hot and dense with temperatures exceeding billions of degrees. Afterwards, the universe cooled. This means that before, the universe was just a mass of heat, so it occurred from so much heat and density that it had gathered up which caused an explosion. Now, millions of years later, the universe is still expanding and cooling from the explosion Of course, the Big Bang might not have happened. The universe could have been born from a huge cloud of dust. The sun, planets, and other bodies formed after the cloud collapsed under gravity. With different abilities, scientists probably consider the Big Bang more accurate than a huge cloud of dust. Scientists have been able to model the universe back to 10^{43} seconds after the Big Bang. This ability proves information that supports the Big Bang to be true. [*She makes the transition here by using the word "although."*]

Although the universe may seem like a big blue sky with the sun, earth, and other planets, it is much more complicated than that, as you can see. There are stars, meteors, comets, planets, and of course, the Earth. Here on Earth, scientists continue to research how the universe began. Is the Big Bang theory really true? The only remains of the original fireball from the Big Bang explosion are faint radio waves. Scientists are searching for a theory that merges quantum mechanics and gravity, but haven't found one yet. They hope the string theory will tie together gravity and quantum mechanics to help them explore further back in time to reveal the truth. With all the theories in the world, there are many different answers to how the universe began. This big question, "How did the universe start?" still awaits a final answer. [*Kathryn concludes by using Connecting Beginning and End.*]

Grade 7: Ben's Research-Based Persuasive Essay

Airbags

Airbags should be optional in vehicles. People should be able to decide whether or not they would like to have an airbag in their car for themselves as well as for their passengers. Airbags do save lives in a really serious accident but they also can kill and seriously injure people in minor accidents. If a car is involved in a minor accident and the airbag deploys, a small person or a child can be more injured by the airbag. [*Ben begins his report by using the Right to the Point strategy. We know exactly what his position is on this issue.*]

In testing, only one size crash dummy has been used. The National Highway Transportation Safely Administration (NHTSA) will soon "require testing with a whole family of crash dummies". ("Safe Airbags or No Airbags"). The NHTSA writes about a small amount of deaths and a large amount of lives saved by airbags but the actual number of deaths is higher and there are huge numbers of severe injuries. "Over 3 million airbags have been recalled in the United States." ("Bag the Mandate"). [*Ben transitions by using Repeat a Related Word and Repeat a Word. Instead of repeating "deaths," he substitutes "being killed." In addition, he uses "severe injuries" ("seriously injured") to connect the two paragraphs.*]

People that are most at risk by being killed or seriously injured by their airbags are drivers who cannot sit 10" back from their airbag because they are short and children under the age of 12. Pregnant women are also at risk. "Rear-facing infant seats must always be placed in the back seat." ("Why Some People Are At Risk").

In 1995 the NHTSA agreed to let people who were at certain risk install on-off switches for both the driver's side and passenger's side of their vehicles. After people apply for this authorization, it can be difficult to find companies to install the on-off switches. A mobile unit will come to your house and install the switch right in your driveway if you can't find anyone to do it.

I have always thought that airbags should be optional in vehicles but now, after learning so much about the danger they carry, I am even more convinced that each driver should have the option about airbags. I am too young to drive but I am usually a passenger in the front seat and wish that I had the choice about whether or not I had an airbag in front of me that might be more harmful than helpful. Airbags should be optional in all vehicles. [*Ben used Connect Beginning and End to conclude his essay. He circles back to his original idea and expands on it a bit before using the same words in the last sentence as he used in the first one. In this case, we think this proved very effective.*]

Works Cited

"Bag the Mandate." 2001. Detroit News Online. 15 February 2000. http://www.detnews.com/EDITPAGE/0002/15/1edit/1edit.htm

"Why Some People Are At Risk." 2001. NHTSA Online. 28 March 2001. http://www.nhtsa.dot.gov/airbags/brochure/

Brown, Robert. "Safe Airbags or No Airbags." NHTSA Online. 2001. 30 March 2000. http://www.airbagsonoff.com/new_page_20.htm

List of Strategies
for Transitions, Leads,
and Conclusions

Transitions

Strategies to Connect One Paragraph to Another

1. Repeat a Word
The author uses a word in the last sentence of a paragraph and then again in the first sentence of the next paragraph to link the paragraphs.

2. Use Related Words
This is similar to Repeat a Word, but instead of repeating the exact word, an author may use a related word, often a synonym.

3. End a Paragraph with a Question
The author ends the paragraph with an interesting question and then begins to address this question in a new paragraph.

4. Begin a Paragraph with a Question
The paragraph begins with a question that moves the reader to a new point.

5. Contrast
A new paragraph begins by stating how the main idea of this paragraph is related to, but dissimilar from, the main idea of the last paragraph. Words such as "conversely," "in contrast," or "on the other hand" may be used to signal this shift.

6. "Although"
Writers begin a paragraph with "Although" to let the reader know a different idea is being introduced.

7. "Is Another"

In one paragraph, the author makes an assertion and backs up this statement with supporting details. In the next paragraph, he comes back to this assertion and provides additional supporting evidence. He makes the transition from one paragraph to the next by using the words ". . . is another" or "another . . . is."

8. Appositive

The information that is contained within two commas connects the new ideas to what has preceded them.

9. Several to One

In one paragraph, the author lists several related items. She begins a new paragraph by selecting one item from this list and elaborating on it.

10. Back and Forth

This strategy is used when the author starts with the idea developed in the last paragraph and switches to a new, related idea.

11. Command

Each new paragraph begins with a verb that moves the reader along from one directive to the next. Words such as "Look," "Check out," "See," and "Take a close look" may be used.

12. Same Start

The author begins consecutive paragraphs with the same carefully crafted words.

Structures That Connect Ideas Throughout the Entire Text

1. Description

The author paints a picture of one event, one person, one time in history and the like. All the details in the report clarify and expand this picture.

2. Moving Through Time (Sequence)

Each paragraph moves the reader along chronologically. Words such as "Five years later," "Not until 1775," or "By the turn of the century" may be used.

3. Compare and Contrast

The paragraphs are structured so that the author can identify how topics are similar and different.

4. Cause and Effect

The author identifies a result (effect) and what led to this result (cause).

5. Explanation
The writer clarifies why something happened or how something works.

Leads

1. Question
The author begins the report by posing a thought-provoking, open-ended question.

2. "Imagine"
The author hooks the reader by drawing him directly into a scene that evokes another time, place, or situation. The word "imagine" often occurs in this lead.

3. Guess Who or What?
The author immediately snatches the reader's attention by inviting him to solve a riddle.

4. Common Reaction
With this strategy, the author begins with a generally held impression of her topic.

5. Right to the Point
The author begins with one short, clear, declarative sentence that states the main idea. The curt statement begs for a fuller explanation, which is found in the remainder of the report.

6. Series of Intriguing Questions
The writer provides a series of well-designed, open-ended questions that may appear to be unconnected. The questions urge the reader on, setting up the expectation that the questions will be answered and that the relationship that ties them together will be revealed.

7. Question and Two-Word Questions
The author begins by asking one major question and then breaks this question down into a series of two-word subquestions.

8. Hanging On
The author provides a series of clues, which the reader uses to uncover the identity of the topic.

9. Past to Present
The author makes a connection with the past. He notes how things once were and then moves to the present.

10. Indisputable Fact
The writer leads off with a statement that is unquestionable; one with which everyone could agree.

11. What's Wrong?
There is a problem. The author clearly identifies it in the lead sentence.

12. Anecdote
The writer shares a short story that relates to the report's topic.

13. Inside Someone's Head
With this strategy, the author reveals what someone or something is thinking.

14. What's Being Done?
The lead immediately introduces the reader to the issue at hand and the step(s) taken to address the issue.

15. Paradox (Something That Goes Against Common Sense)
With this strategy, there appears to be a contradiction between what has been written and what we believe to be true.

Conclusions

1. Dreaming of the Future
The article concludes with the author wondering about future possibilities for his topic.

2. Posing a Question
The author asks a thought-provoking question to get the reader to continue to think about the topic after the piece has been read.

3. Ask a Question and Answer It
The author concludes by asking a question and then supplying the answer in the same paragraph.

4. "Although"
The author ends the paper or report by contrasting a piece of information with the main point of the article. The first word of this conclusion is "although."

5. "Finally"
Many writers signal the end of their piece by beginning the last paragraph with the word "finally."

6. Help!
The author lets the reader know that help is needed.

7. No Doubt About It!
The author ends the piece by drawing one indisputable conclusion about her topic. Phrases such as "One thing seems certain," "Without a doubt," or "There is no question" may signal the use of this strategy.

8. Giving Advice
The author ends the piece by providing a bit of advice or a suggestion.

9. Sharing an Emotion
The author describes the emotional effect the topic has had on him.

10. What's Next?
The author concludes by telling the reader what the final step in a sequence of events will be.

11. Right Now
The author concludes by bringing the reader up-to-date. He describes the topic's current condition, often using the word "today" to signal this strategy.

12. "No Matter" Plus Draw a Conclusion
The author begins with the words "No matter." Next she draws a conclusion.

13. Providing a Summary
The author recaps the key points in the article or report in the last paragraph.

14. Connecting Beginning and End
The author connects information from the first paragraph to information in the final paragraph. Often the same words are repeated in both parts of the report or article.

15. Quote
The author finds an appropriate quote from her research that can bring closure to the piece.

References

Bastian, K. R. K. 1997. "Animal Mummies." *Muse* 1 (1): 8–12.

Beck, I. L., M. G. McKeown, R. L. Hamilton, and L. Kucan. 1997. *Questioning the Author: An Approach for Enhancing Student Engagement with Text.* Newark, DE: International Reading Association.

Bergin, D. A., and C. LaFave. 1998. "Continuities Between Motivation Research and Whole Language Philosophy of Instruction." *Journal of Literacy Research,* 30 (3): 321–56.

Brudick, T. 1997. "Snakes and Snails and Puppy Dog Tails: Girls and Boys Expressing Voice in Information Research Projects." *Journal of Youth Services in Libraries,* 11 (1): 28–36.

Chaney, A. L., and T. L. Burk. 1998. *Teaching Oral Communication in Grades K–8.* Boston: Allyn & Bacon.

Clemmons, J., and L. Laase. 1995. *Language Arts Mini-Lessons: Step-by-Step Skill-Builders for Your Classroom.* New York: Scholastic.

Collard, S. B., III. 1992. *Do They Scare You? Creepy Creatures.* Watertown, MA: Charlesbridge.

Cooney, B. 1996. *Eleanor.* New York: Viking.

Dell, N. 2000. "3.6 Minutes Per Day: The Scarcity of Informational Texts in Grade 1." *Reading Research Quarterly,* 35 (2), 202–24.

Devine, T. G. 1987. *Teaching Study Skills: A Guide for Teachers, 2d ed.* Boston: Allyn & Bacon.

Georgia Department of Education Writing Assessment. Retrieved December 14, 2001 from www.doe.K12.ga.US/sla/ret/writing.html.

Gillin, J. 2002. Re-Modeling: Revising Expository Writing. Paper presented at the National Council of Teachers of English Spring Conference, March, Portland, Oregon.

Graves, D. H. 1992. "Helping Students Learn to Read Their Portfolios." In *Portfolio Portraits,* ed. D. H. Graves and B. S. Sunstein. Portsmouth, NH: Heinemann.

Gunning, T. G. 1998. *Assessing and Correcting Reading and Writing Difficulties.* Boston: Allyn & Bacon.

Harvey, S. 1998. *Nonfiction Matters: Reading, Writing and Research in Grades 3–8.* Portland, ME: Stenhouse.

Hayes, J. R., R. E. Young, M. L. Matchett, M. McCaffrey, C. Cochran, and T. Hajduk. 1992. "Writing from Sources." In *Reading Empirical Research Studies. The Rhetoric of Research,* ed. J. R. Hayes, R. E. Young, M. L. Matchett, M. McCaffrey, C. Cochran, and T. Hajduk, pp. 467–68. Hillsdale, NJ: Lawrence Erlbaum.

Idaho Department of Education Bureau of Curriculum and Accountability —Statewide testing. Retrieved January 4, 2002 from www.sde.id.US/instruct/Statewidetest.htm.

Kuhlthau, C. C. 1988. "Developing a Model of the Library Search Process: Cognitive and Affective Aspects." *Research Quarterly,* 28 (2): 232–43.

———. 1994. *Teaching the Library Research Process. 2d ed.* Metuchen, NJ: The Scarecrow Press.

Laase, L. 1997. "Study Skills." *Instructor* (May/June): 58.

Lane, B. 1993. *After the End: Teaching and Learning Creative Revision.* Portsmouth, NH: Heinemann.

Lukeman, N. 2000. *The First Five Pages: A Writer's Guide to Staying Out of the Recycle Pile.* New York: Simon & Schuster.

Mabry, L. 1999. "Writing to the Rubric" [Electronic version]. *Phi Delta Kappan,* 80 (9), 673–79.

Massachusetts English Language Arts Curriculum Framework. 2001. Malden, MA: Massachusetts Department of Education.

McGregor, J. H. 1994. "Cognitive Processes and the Use of Information: A Qualitative Study of Higher-Order Thinking Skills Used in the Research Process by Students in a Gifted Program." In *School Library Media Annual 12,* ed. C. C. Kuhlthau, pp. 124–33.

Nelson, J., and J. R. Hayes. 1988. *How the Writing Context Shapes College Students' Strategies for Writing from Sources.* Technical Report No. 16. Berkeley, CA: Center for the Study of Writing (ERIC Document Reproduction Service No. ED 297374).

O'Brien, P. 2000. *The Hindenburg.* New York: Henry Holt.

Ogle, D. 1986. "K-W-L: A Teaching Model That Develops Active Reading of Expository Text." *The Reading Teacher,* 39: 564–70.

Ohio Department of Education. *The Ninth-Grade Proficiency Test in Writing: A Resource Manual for Teachers of Writing.* Columbus, Ohio (ERIC Document Reproduction Service No. ED 443122).

Pearson, P. D., and M. C. Gallagher. 1983. "The Instruction of Reading Comprehension." *Contemporary Educational Psychology,* 8: 317–44.

Peters, P. 1985. *Strategies for Student Writers: A Guide to Writing Essays, Tutorial Papers, Exam Papers and Reports.* Chichester, UK: Wiley.

Ploeger, K. M. 2000. *Simplified Paragraph Skills.* Lincolnwood, IL: NTC Publishing Group.

Raphael, T. E. 1986. "Teaching Question Answer Relationships, Revisited." *The Reading Teacher,* 40: 516–22.

Rief, L. 1999. *Vision and Voice: Extending the Literacy Spectrum.* Portsmouth, NH: Heinemann.

Roth, A. 1989. *The Research Paper: Process, Form and Content. 6th ed.* Belmont, CA: Wadsworth.

Routman, R. 2000. *Conversations: Strategies for Teaching, Learning, and Evaluating.* Portsmouth, NH: Heinemann.

Schirmer, B. R., and J. Bailey. 2000. "Writing Assessment Rubric: An Instructional Approach with Struggling Writers." *TEACHING Exceptional Children,* 33 (1): 52–58.

Schwegler, R. A., and L. K. Shamoon. 1982. "The Aims and Process of the Research Paper." *College English,* 44: 817–24.

Sebranek, P., V. Meyer, and D. Kemper. 1995. *Write Source 2000.* Burlington, WI: Write Source Educational.

Short, K. G., J. Schroeder, J. Laird, G. Kauffman, M. J. Ferguson, and K. M. Crawford. 1996. *Learning Together Through Inquiry: From Columbus to Integrated Curriculum.* Portland, ME: Stenhouse.

Siegel, B., and M. McMackin. 2000. "Researching: Merging Inquiry and Writing." *Currents in Literacy,* 3 (1): 1, 4–7.

Silverman, J., E. Hughes, and D. R. Wienbroer. 1999. *Rules of Thumb: A Guide for Writers, 4th ed.* Boston: McGraw-Hill.

Simon, L. 1988. *Good Writing: A Guide and Sourcebook for Writing Across the Curriculum.* New York: St. Martin's Press.

Spandel, V., and R. Culham. No date. 702 Observing and Reporting: Expository Writing. Retrieved December 29, 2001, from http://intranet.cps.k12.il.us/Assessments/Ideas_and_Rubrics_Bank/rubric_bank.html.

Spandel, V., and R. Stiggins. 1997. *Creating Writers: Linking Writing Assessment and Instruction.* New York: Longman.

Spivey, N. N. 1985. Discourse Synthesis: Constructing Texts in Reading and Writing. Unpublished Ph.D. diss., University of Texas at Austin.

Tower, C. 2000. "Questions That Matter: Preparing Elementary Students for the Inquiry Process." *The Reading Teacher,* 53 (7): 550–57.

Tracey, K. 1997. *Teaching Freshmen to Understand Research as a Process of Inquiry* (ERIC Document Reproduction Service No. 414596).

Vacca, R. T., and J. L. Vacca. 1993. *Content Area Reading, 4th ed.* New York: HarperCollins.

Wasserstein, P. 2001. "I Don't Know What Happened—Johnny Used to Love Writing." *Understanding Our Gifted,* 13 (2): 13–15.